The No Contact Rule

NATALIE LUE

Published by Naughty Girl Media

Natalie Lue asserts the moral right to be identified as the author of this work.

Copyright 2013 Natalie Lue

Cover design by Lulabird Creative.

This is the first print edition of this book and the second edition in digital format. This edition is in British English.

ISBN: 146639577X
ISBN-13: 9781466395770

For B.

CONTENTS

MY STORY

When I finally decided to cut contact with a Mr Unavailable (emotionally unavailable man) who also had a girlfriend, I also had the unfortunate predicament of working with him. Unlike all the other times when I'd told him it was over – had yelled, and ranted, raved, and no doubt shrieked like a banshee - this time, it was done with no fanfare simply because I couldn't take the embarrassment of yet another thing I'd sworn that I didn't follow through with.

After overhearing him cooking up an alibi with my friend's boyfriend outside my bedroom door, I suddenly realised that after eighteen months of bullshit, I'd had *enough* and that not only was he most definitely not 'my man' but that I would rather be miserable on my own. Despite the fact that he could offer me no more now than the day we'd become involved, he had a huge stranglehold over my life. Emotionally, and even healthwise, I'd hit rock bottom.

Breakups are bad enough and when you have to do it with a work colleague, it's even trickier but for the sake of my sanity and for my own self-respect, I just *had* to cut contact and distance myself from him. First came me saying that I was busy for lunch, shocking him as we used to have lunch together as often as possible. Then followed me saying that I was busy that evening and ignoring his calls and texts. Of course emails followed and what with us working together we crossed paths, but I kept myself distant and polite, and tried not to get drawn into anything. Without realising it, I was attempting to teach him that I wasn't going to do what he expected anymore – instead it would be a case of No Contact and setting boundaries, although I didn't even know that this is what it was. It was instinct, gut and self-preservation.

It's also important to note that as we weren't in a 'proper' relationship – after all it's pretty difficult to break up with someone who's already in a relationship with someone else – I had no choice but to let my *actions* do the talking. I'd kept waiting for him to do the decent thing and spare me from any more pain by walking away but I realised, he was *never* going to do the decent thing; I had to do it.

The following week, I'm pretty sure that he expected things to return to normal, but they didn't, and week after week after week passed. At times it was agonising. I'd pace my flat close to tearing my hair out as I wondered if I'd made a mistake, whether I'd been too hasty, too demanding, too a lot of things, but I gradually realised that I didn't miss the drama and feeling like second best and cold turkeyed it out.

The times when I was tempted to cave often coincided with something else stressing me, or the sting of rejection making me want to avoid the truth of our involvement. I didn't want to *see* myself. Reaching out seemed like the perfect solution because I'd fantasise that he was afraid of getting in touch with me because I'd cut contact with him. I'd imagine that I would get in touch and he'd be delighted to hear from me, apologise profusely and announce that he was going to leave his girlfriend. But, every time these thoughts crossed my mind, I'd remember not one, not two, but countless examples where he'd disappointed me and I just couldn't face feeling that way again.

It was hard and along the way there were several major confrontations, normally caused by him getting drunk at an event, getting jealous, professing his love and then admitting that his situation hadn't changed.

Just before lunch one day, he managed to catch me on my own and quizzed me about a guy from work who I'd had an entirely innocent conversation with.

"I'm not talking about this. I've told you to leave me alone!" and I walked away from him. Feeling a bit deflated, I decided to go to Pret a Manger and grab some lunch. I admit I was wondering if I was being too harsh on him. Heading back to the office, I froze, open mouthed in shock, when I spotted this fool coming out of our building with a bunch of flowers walking towards his girlfriend *less than ten minutes* after he'd accosted me. It was all I could do not to grab those flowers and ram them up his arse!

This incident toughened me up and restored my resolve. It also no doubt helped to limit the pain when I bumped into him in a club while I was out with a group of friends – including a platonic male friend from work. He threw a major tantrum and accused me of all sorts of things, only for me to see him a while later dancing with his girlfriend (who I hadn't known was there) and she had on an *engagement ring*.

I moved on to someone else (another Mr Unavailable but there's a whole other book on that) which admittedly helped to distract from the hurt. When I finished it with him, I spent more time focusing on me and managed to avoid falling off the wagon a few times... and then I finally did, almost a year after starting No Contact. I instantly regretted it and got right back on the NC saddle.

I could have agonised over what had, in effect lasted all of a few hours, but I realised that while I would have preferred not to have slipped up, the experience had actually only cemented my reasons for cutting contact in the first place. It empowered me to continue and move on. I didn't have to wonder "What if?" or ponder the *Coulda, Woulda, Shouldas*. And from that moment onwards, what little power he thought he'd had evaporated. I never looked back because I knew what was there.

I knew that I was no longer No Contact and was in fact just Living My Life when one day it occurred to me that I'd stopped anticipating whether he'd get in touch or wondering what was going on with him and his girlfriend.

To be quite frank, I just didn't give a shit anymore. He knew it too – his attempts were becoming half-hearted and he was increasingly wary of creating more conflict. He ended up having to see me with dates at social engagements where we had mutual friends, and to eventually see me happy with someone else. This was major progress considering that I'd believed that I couldn't be happy with anyone else and that he was my 'last chance' at love when I'd first initiated No Contact. I mistook the source of my misery for also being the sole source of my happiness.

One of the things that I learned through being in a number of relationships and cutting contact was that in or out of the relationship, I was creating my own pain. I'm not saying he or any of my other exes weren't doing what *they* were doing, but in terms of how long I stuck around, what I put up with, how receptive I was, and my *own* relationship habits, *that* was all me. This turned out to be very empowering knowledge because I realised that I could also be in charge of creating my own happiness.

He's not the only man I've had to cut contact with; my past is littered with texts, emails, letters, dropped calls, instant messages, voicemails, and nostalgic calls that I've either fallen for, or had to ignore for the sake of my own sanity. My life has moved on dramatically since those days, but every day through my blog Baggage Reclaim (www.baggagereclaim.com) and also my book, *Mr Unavailable and the Fallback Girl*, I still help thousands of people recognise that they have to cut contact and teach the object of their misguided affections to expect something different from them, so that they can move on and be free of destructive relationships.

I've written *The No Contact Rule* because there are so many people trying to work their way out of the pain and gain some understanding about their situation. I only wish that I'd known then what I know now and this book will support you through this difficult time. This is inspired entirely by what I learned through my own experiences as well as those of the many thousands of readers I've come across and helped over the past eight years. While your pain is unique to you, take some comfort from the fact that the situations, when they're boiled down, are very much the same.

Many people have said that I've acted like the friend they wish would talk straight with them and this is my no holds barred guide to understanding the act of cutting contact with someone who you just can't seem to break up from.

If you fear the pain of breaking up and are also afraid of what you may or may not do when confronted with certain situations when you think you might be helpless or weak, this book is for you.

If you're afraid that they might suddenly change and you won't be there to reap the benefits, this book is *definitely* for you.

Breaking up can be tough but it's gotta be done to sever ties with a relationship that's not working. You also cannot treat yourself with love, care, trust and respect if you remain in a situation that depletes you of these things. Nor can you open the door to better times and a better relationship if you don't close the door on this relationship and stop looking back. At some point, and better sooner rather than later, you've got to move forwards and allow the distance to grow between this situation and you. That time is now.

MODERN WORLD, MODERN BREAKUP

Back in 'olden times', which is basically the time before mobile phones, email, online dating, instant messaging, Facebook, Twitter, LinkedIn etc, breakups were still hard but a lot simpler. If someone wanted to dip in and out of your life at will, they kinda had to put in a lot more effort, as technology didn't give them the type of lazy access that so many enjoy in today's modern dating world. Yep, you heard me right – *lazy* access.

I love technology but I don't like its impact on dating, especially as it makes the emotionally distant, lazy and opportunistic even *more* distant, lazy and opportunistic, allowing them to play havoc with the lives of the people they're involved with by creating an illusion of interest that doesn't exist, or at least not to the level that we believe it to be. In olden times you could quickly differentiate between effort and *crumbs.* When you broke, you *broke,* and if you wanted to know what they were doing (and vice versa), you had to pick up the phone, send a letter or lurk around outside their home, work or around their friends.

Many modern breakups are ambiguous and tortuous because we can remain connected to an ex in so many ways and there's all this 'let's be friends', 'let's touch base', 'I don't want to look immature by defriending' and other such bullshit. Next thing you know, months or even years have gone by and it occurs to you that your life hasn't moved on because you've been too busy dealing with an ex, who incidentally, may even have started their *own* new relationship in the meantime. We're now so casual about relationships that some people don't even want to date, they want to *casually date* and then some want to have a *casual breakup* where they pretty much get to continue on as is *without* the commitment.

Breakups are about ending relationships and what many people are afraid of is actually breaking, letting go and moving on.

I've heard from so many people who are struggling with breakups because they can't bear the idea of being done, even if it's so done, it's like trying to breathe life back into a corpse. It's never been more acceptable to manage down your expectations and to essentially keep offering up everything but the kitchen sink in the hope that the person will change their mind and decide to love you and commit. There's this fear of finality and there's definitely a pervasive fear of getting it wrong and losing out on your 'investment'. It's being scared that you're never going to speak to them again or that you're going to be forgotten, the fear that you've misjudged a situation (that you've actually judged correctly), and the fear that they might spontaneously combust into a better person in a better relationship... without you.

This is why so many *want* to breakup but just end up leaving their proverbial door open so that their ex can keep their foot in it just in case it turns out to be a mistake. But this also positions them as a *backup option*.

Breaking up is hard and while there are a number of factors that can make it difficult, like low self-esteem or the other party not respecting your wishes, the pain is felt mostly by people who are unable to recognise that they have to suffer the short, possibly even medium-term pain to feel the long-term gain. This is made even more difficult when you're actually trying to move on but the other party won't leave you alone. This means you don't get the chance to grieve the relationship so that you *can* move on. In fact, you're likely to deduce that if they're still sniffing around, it's because they want the relationship as much as you do, they just don't know how to go about it.

I'm not saying that breakups weren't difficult back in the day, but our parents, for example, did not have to put up with half of the bullshit manoeuvres that we do, simply because societal acceptance of casual relationships and technology weren't there to be taken advantage of. They may have discussed things, decided to end it and then gone their separate ways. If one of the parties wanted to pursue, they had to pick up the phone, write a letter or, heaven forbid, get on foot and go and see them face-to-face. Their options were limited whereas now, there are too many options that enable people to dodge *real* communication.

The modern-day breakup is now accompanied by a series of lazy communication manoeuvres that don't really communicate very much at all other than the fact that the person sending them is lazy and scared, and that they perceive the person on the receiving end to be 'low maintenance'. From my own experiences and those of readers, it's clear that after a series of discussions, the breakup happens, then the one line texts, or tentative emails, or calls at 2 am in the morning start. I have readers telling me how they end up staring at a text or email for *hours* trying to decipher what was meant and why it was sent. I kid you not when I say that some of these texts say stuff like "Great match tonight"; "I hope you're not still mad at me..."; "How crap is this weather today?"; "Check out this joke...{lame joke follows}" and even "Hi".

After months of hearing nothing, a random, often pathetic joke email or text turns up and this is supposed to trigger something from the recipient. Unfortunately, often it *does*, because this 'new way' of doing things has us believing that attention is attention. Often we're so excited to hear something, *anything* from the person we've been involved with, that we don't stop and think about the *quality* of this attention and what their latest behaviour means in the wider context of the relationship.

I'm going to be real with you; if you were going out with a semi-decent person, they'd have enough empathy to realise that when people break up, they need a little, or even a lot, of space to have a chance to breathe,

grieve the relationship and get over it.

They're the type, if told that they should leave you be for a while, they'll respect your wishes, whereas the type of person that you need to cut contact with has *no empathy* for what you are experiencing and is focused on what suits them. It doesn't necessarily mean that they're *incapable* of empathy but what it does mean is that it's not something that they employ due to making themselves the centre of their universe and yours. It's all about making themselves comfortable and their attitude is that *they* feel OK with your relationship as it is, so ipso facto you should too. Or they reason that because *they're* uncomfortable with you blanking them that you should make them feel better about it by not cutting contact, or by giving them sex or whatever. This means that even though they have nothing further to offer you, possibly even *less* than before, they'll still poke around in your life because they *want* to.

They assume that you're sitting around, eating ice cream by the tub, sobbing into your tea and biscuits and struggling to get through the day waiting for them to dignify you with some level of contact. Unfortunately, often you are and it's time to shake things up.

We also have to accept that we can be just as willing to engage in, or even *start* lazy communication while seeking attention and validation, and modern breakups seem to involve a hell of a lot of ambiguity as well as the likes of sex, virtual sex and even trying to continue the relationship unofficially. It's all too easy to get involved in game playing and yes, passive aggression in the form of appearing to go along with an ex's agenda while having our *own* agenda that we're really trying to get pushed through. Next thing you know, our expectations have been managed *right* down.

Modern dating has taught many of us to expect crumbs and to believe that the crumbs are a loaf, when in actual fact, they're just crumbs. NC

puts an end to all of these shenanigans.

Depending on how we have been raised or our experiences in adult relationships, we have our own idea of what we think love or a relationship is, and for some of us, those beliefs are not very healthy. The fundamental problem derailing self-esteem and relationships is a lack of boundaries; we either have none or very little, or we don't enforce them. You'll hear the term 'boundaries' a lot throughout this book because 1) you need them for yourself and 2), you need them for whoever you're cutting contact with and in *all* of your relationships because boundaries teach people what you will and won't accept and also teach them how to treat you.

No Contact establishes boundaries, something I can assure you that you desperately need.

Think of **boundaries** as **your personal electric fence** that allows you to actively decide what you will and won't accept while also enabling you to ensure that you're living your life in accordance with your *own* values – the things that you believe that you need in order to live your life happily and authentically. Boundaries set limits. NC is opting out due to having reached your limit and then some.

A breakup inadvertently creates a boundary that draws a line between you both. It's not the case that everyone breaks up because something bad happens but boundaries do help you to recognise how you want to feel or not feel in a relationship, and how you want to be treated. By breaking up, a new boundary is created that communicates that the relationship you had is over and the privileges and fringe benefits that you've both previously enjoyed are now over too. If you've broken up, you cannot continue to behave in the way that you have. You can't expect, need or want to the same levels. Otherwise, how is the other party supposed to recognise and understand that it's over so that they can move on? How are *you* supposed to move on in body, mind and spirit? Of course you're going to struggle emotionally with a breakup if your *actions* are not communicating that the relationship is *over*.

Tempting as it may be, you cannot have your cake and eat it too. Someone will get the short end of the stick and if you're contemplating cutting contact, that person is *you*.

- You can't say it's over and then try to control who they see, what they do and where they go.
- You can't say it's over and then get mad if they get involved with someone else or start getting on with their life sooner than you do.
- *They* can't expect to not meet your needs but still keep creeping back expecting the same fringe benefits.
- *They* can't say that they want out but then keep you in their back pocket as a rainy day option.

You'll quickly discover when you have no boundaries and you stay or keep taking your ex back, that they become the person of diminishing returns – you're doing the same as before or even more and getting even less back while they reap the rewards. This is the fundamental problem with your relationships because you need to adjust your needs, expectations and wants to align with the fact that the relationship isn't working and it's *supposed* to be ending. But *they* also need to realise that they cannot enjoy the same access that they had while in the relationship, *outside* of it.

Often the people who require NC are the type that want your emotions, ego stroking, a shag and a shoulder to lean on without the 'trappings' of a relationship.

People are getting away with things that they could not have gotten away with before, and it's partly down to making use of lazy communication methods like texts, emails and Facebook, but it's also because they *can*. All that's happened is that their options for mucking you around have expanded plus the social consequences of not being in a relationship or even getting married have significantly lessened over the past couple of decades in particular. They engage in lazy communication because they want to know that you're *still* there and often you're only too eager to let them know that you still are.

It took me a long time to realise, but there are certain types of people out there that can't commit – they can't commit to being with you and they can't commit to *not* being with you. Don't let the first time you truly realise and accept this truth be when you've already devoted your entire life to trying to make somebody like this do otherwise.

Commitment resisters are the 'driver' in their relationships - they're the one with more power and they set the terms. Even though you as the passenger will no doubt have your own commitment issues, the lack of power directly affects the way that you behave as you're curtailed by the driver. They do *exactly* what suits them without real care or thought for how it affects you. They do things on their terms. Even though they may make insincere noises of care and concern, their priorities are getting a shag, an ego stroke or a shoulder to lean on for sounding off, or all three of these. They also get 'turned on' by absence and are obsessed with feeling the heady rush of desire created by 'beginnings' and also by the panic that follows when someone doesn't dance to their beat, leaving them out of control.

They'll flip flop around you, hanging around like an irritating scab, dipping in and out of your life but keeping a firm foothold in it, because they need the security of knowing that there is at least *one* person out there wanting them, that they can default to or rely on.

In their mind, you're broken up with an option to cash in a credit should the need arise, on the basis that you'll be ready and willing should they need you. I've heard so many stories of people abandoning new and far healthier relationships, including engagements and marriages because an ex that they should be steering clear of is suddenly lurking around, promising a future and a change in themselves that just *isn't* going to materialise. It's incredibly painful for the people who leave because they allow themselves to be lured away on 'chemistry', 'history', sex, promises or their ego that needs to 'win' and then they feel like a cruel joke has been played on them and lament the relationship or even personal happiness that they threw away for, in essence, a gamble.

Due to the lack of restrictions we impose on ourselves in modern relationships and also our eagerness to quickly move on and avoid our feelings, unavailable relationships are highly prevalent.

In 'olden times' it was more evident if you hadn't moved on. Now *lots* of people haven't moved on and are soothing themselves with people whom they've appointed as their own personal emotional airbags. There just isn't that same *pressure* anymore to be committed in the way that it would have been, for instance, in our parents' time. We like to leave the door open 'just in case'; we have a lot of loose ends, and if we're entirely honest with ourselves, we get too caught up in worrying about how things look and protecting our egos instead of how things *are* and our happiness. We make ourselves powerless and resign ourselves to more of a bad deal because we prefer the familiar uncomfortable to the unknown uncomfortable.

You're scared to break up, scared of dealing with them when they get back in touch, scared that maybe they're going to change into something amazing after you let them go, and scared that you may be alone and scared *to* be alone. If you need to cut contact with someone, it's likely that you have some love habits that are contributing to what can certainly feel like a vicious cycle.

The No Contact Rule is your no-holds-barred guide to telling that person to take a run and jump or at the very least to step right back and let you have some personal space without actually having to utter the words. More importantly, *The No Contact Rule* is about taking back your power and taking care of your *own* needs. Understand why it's difficult to walk away and what types of situations make you more prone to needing No Contact to discover what you ultimately need to do in order to move on healthily with your self-esteem in tow.

I hear from people who have broken up *fifty times*. FIFTY. I hear from people who are trying to figure out how to cut off an ex from their life that they broke up with one, two or even *three* decades ago. I'm hearing from people who are knocking on retirement whose lives are literally coming apart due to the 'torture' of snooping on Facebook or an email affair that didn't come to fruition.

You only have one life to lead – you have better things to do with your time and your emotions than remaining tied to someone who does not truly *value* you.

Yes this book is about breakups but it's even more about empowering yourself so that you can close the door on this relationship and ultimately be available for something more befitting of you. A relationship that requires NC is not doing you justice.

In this time where you are wide open to so many more opportunities to hear from somebody or see what's going on in their life without actually *being* in their lives, having a period of space after a breakup is even more vital. In a world which is excessively concerned with image, it's all too easy to fall into the trap of spending far too much time worrying about how you look on Facebook or how you're going to be perceived by mutual friends or 'everyone' and whether you're a 'meanie', when in actual fact your breakup needs to be have boundaries and you have to manage *your* feelings and ensure that you maintain a healthy self-image. Being a people pleaser will cripple it.

Learn how to break up with people that don't want to break and let you go so that you can live a better life and be a person with higher self-esteem. Learn how to step away even when you don't want to step away despite the negative impact on your life. *The No Contact Rule* is the quick guide to avoiding being an option for someone to default to or 'fall back on' as a rainy day option while contributing little or nothing, as well as helping you to exit out of situations where you're at best being taken advantage of, and at worst being abused. Regardless of what has happened in or out of the relationship, this is also about coming out of an involvement or relationship with your dignity intact because if you see yourself as 'broken' every time you go through a breakup, this has a knock-on effect with your future involvements as well.

Break up from a depleting relationship with dignity but remember, you need to accept that it's going to hurt for a while. But that will pass. Stop fearing the pain!

UNDERSTANDING NC & ASSESSING YOUR SITUATION

GETTING TO GRIPS WITH THE CONCEPT OF NO CONTACT

It's pretty damn painful to find yourself in the position of having to consider cutting contact with someone, especially when you're either still crazy about them, or you used to believe that they were the centre of the universe. Understandably this is a position that nobody wants to be in but the reality is that you are, and the longer that you fight it, the more you prolong the agony, the further you are from actually getting on with your own life and feeling happy again.

The likelihood is that you've tried things the nice, normal way and it hasn't worked – the 'traditional' breakup. This is where one or both of you recognise things aren't working; you might have had a series of discussions or even clashes and tentatively broached the subject of breaking up. You may have given it more time or one or both of you agreed that it was time to end it. You're both upset, you probably both say that you're going to be friends, speak periodically over the few weeks to a month after you break up to arrange to return possessions, to check on each other (neither of you will admit it's to make yourselves feel less 'guilty'), you may even have one or a few last shags for old time's sake, and then you both steer clear of one another to grieve the relationship and get on with your respective lives. You may even have agreed that you'll leave each other alone for a while, but ultimately it's a respectful breakup. It doesn't feel like you left behind everything including your dignity and self-esteem.

17

No Contact (NC and also known as the No Contact Rule/NCR) is the **boundary building actions** that come into place post-breakup and is especially useful to people who have lost credibility during a relationship, or afterwards, because their own actions and words don't match.

NC is a means of **mentally, emotionally and physically distancing yourself from somebody** so that you can gain perspective, grieve the loss of the relationship and take back control of yourself and rebuild your life so that you can move on. You give yourself space and time to do this by eradicating/limiting all of your contact with the other person so that you can face the loss without disruption that will otherwise set you back and potentially keep you stuck in a cycle of unhealthy behaviour.

By going NC you **change what has been your typical habits with this person or even in your relationships in general** and the time you take and what you do with it, will **neutralise the effect of this person** and your involvement as well as improve your self-esteem.

NC means literally that - so no texts, calls, email, letters, IM, Facebook, Twitter, LinkedIn snooping, no tapping up mutual friends for information about them, no sex, no meeting up, no attention seeking. Basically avoiding anything that keeps you in emotional, spiritual and physical contact with them.

NC makes you **unavailable to your ex so that you can get**

over the breakup and build your self-esteem back up to become emotionally, physically and spiritually available for a relationship that befits you.

No Contact is what I like to think of as the last resort. So you've tried the traditional breakup route, possibly on a number of occasions with the same person and it didn't work, or due to the nature of your relationship, you already recognise that once you say it's over, for your own sake and possibly theirs, you will need to distance yourself and cut contact.

What NC Isn't

Many people are confused about what No Contact is, with it being viewed as 'punishment', 'the silent treatment', a means of playing a game, or what you do only when someone is a really, really 'bad' person. Now if you think of NC as being any of these things, you're not going to do it because you're either going to feel like a very bad person *yourself*, or you're going to be engaging in manipulative behaviour. Or you're going to either wait until things are 100% bad and dangerous or rationalise that because it's not 'as bad' as whatever you deem to be 'terrible' you have no option but to keep hammering away at doing what already isn't working.

NC isn't punishment

Cutting contact is often seen in one of two misleading ways; self-punishment or punishing the other party. You are most likely to associate NC with you being punished if you tend to see things in terms of your 'worth' or people not doing as you would like them to do as some sort of rejection, so it then becomes a natural next step to think, "I'm in all of this pain and having to make changes and face uncomfortable realisations. I'm being punished and I don't deserve it!"

The pain you're experiencing is a part of extricating yourself from an unhealthy relationship as well as a natural part of grief and loss. Not all pain is punishment and it's unrealistic to expect to exit a relationship that was causing you pain in the first place, without experiencing some pain. What you're feeling isn't about you having done something bad, as if more worthy, deserving people have painless breakups and make difficult decisions and get instant results. You're also not punishing him/her and the only way it becomes punishment is if you use NC to assert your own agenda in the relationship and attempt to grab *their* power and manipulate them into doing what you want.

NC is also going to look like 'punishment' if you use it to lash out at them or you use it to impose some sort of sentence on yourself for effing up. NC is actually a very positive, empowering and self-affirming experience which is all the more reason to take the time to understand it and see the positives, rather than the perceived negatives which may legitimise you remaining in a bad romance and feeling 'helpless'.

NC is not the same as giving someone the silent treatment in a relationship

Silent treatment in a relationship is a form of abuse and manipulation and the only time when NC would cross into this territory is if you were actually doing NC with a view to manipulating them into doing what you want. This isn't NC; it's game-playing.

If someone is not respecting your boundaries in and out of the relationship, continuing to offer yourself and your boundaries up is not going to change the situation and that's still the same case even when you have boundaries, because having them runs counter to their own agenda. They're showing that they're unable to behave with care, trust and respect and you have the right to remove yourself for a time or even permanently.

In healthy relationships, not being in touch after a breakup is something entirely normal and not regarded as the silent treatment. If the other party doesn't hear back, they rightly assume that this person is not in a good place right now and grieving, or that they're trying to move on with their own life and not ready to go there yet. There doesn't have to be any animosity about this and your conscience is clear on the silent treatment front *as long* as NC is with a view to moving on, *not* to coerce them into doing what you want.

It's also important to note that if you have been involved with someone who is quite conscientious, they will *empathise* with your position even if they don't entirely agree with it, and respect that you need the space and time to deal with things in whatever manner you choose. Someone who isn't too caught up in themselves will make the connection between what has occurred and what you're doing and respect the inevitable space that the situation has brought about.

It's not a game

You've already seen game-playing crop up in the first two reasons and that's simply because it tends to be at the heart of misuse and misinterpretation. NC is not the relationship equivalent of a 'Get Rich Quick Scheme' as you're more likely to get hurt quick.

If you're seeking a shortcut to 'make' the person give you the relationship that you want, you're barking up the wrong tree because aside from being childish, it's like obtaining goods by deception and ultimately they *will* do a bait and switch on you, so they will regain control and you will have to play games all over again. You will also never be able to feel confident that the person is there because they want to be and value you, *not* because they were manipulated and coerced into the relationship. Plus, if you know them well enough, you're unlikely to feel confident that they're not playing their own game. It all becomes a bit cat and mouse.

Playing games undermines your credibility and you may be playing a game where you don't even know the rules. If they are someone who at best takes advantage of, or at worst, abuses you, game-playing is like giving them the green light to treat you badly when they already think that they have the 'right' to do so. Don't give them that opportunity.

It's not just for 'really, really bad people'

First of all, one person's idea of a 'bad' person and yours may be two very different things. You're not God, Judge Judy or a higher power – all you have to do is judge the situation even if it means judging yourself out of it. It's not about being 'good' vs 'bad'; it's about recognising that there are certain types of behaviour and situations that, whether it's one thing or twenty things, renders the possibility of a healthy relationship a no-go.

They may have their 'good points', but the truth is, most people do. Even serial killers on death row have people madly in love with them. NC doesn't mean that you have judged the person as 'bad' but what it *does* mean is that you've judged the situation to be unhealthy and impervious to basic boundaries. If you look beyond the moment or the short-term, eventually most people are not in touch with most of their exes. This is normal and called *moving on*. They don't think of it as NC (even if it started that way) – they're just living their lives. Your ex will still be able to go about their life. They're not under some sort of court order or subjected to every man and his dog judging them for whatever has gone down in the relationship. You're not going NC because they're a bad person; you're going NC because you want to move on.

You also have to get over this idea that you don't have the *right* to leave or the *right* to no longer feel that this relationship is meeting your needs, expectations and wishes. There doesn't have to be any 'bad' reason for going NC or just breaking up. Relationships stop working and dates don't work out. You are *entitled* to take the personal space you need to come to terms with your disappointment and the loss of this relationship and to move on. You cannot hold yourself hostage in a cack-handed attempt to live your life by consensus because believe me, when this person is ready to move on or even take their own space, they won't be looking for your permission!

WHEN NC IS MOST APPROPRIATE

1) **When they can't commit but are still trying to maintain you as an option.** This is tough. It's not about them being a 'bad' person but what it is about is recognising that you have needs too and they're *valid* and if they're not able to commit, they're not available for a relationship. Them trying to keep you in their life so that they don't have to commit to that decision and so that they also get the opportunity to take you on in case they change their mind will cripple your self-esteem and any chances of a friendship or even a reconciliation further down the line. When you *break*, you *break*. They can't commit to being with you but they can't commit to *not* being with you either so you have to commit to NC.

2) **When you have low self-esteem.** Again, it's not about the other party being a 'bad' person but if you don't treat yourself with love, care, trust and respect, what someone else is giving you, even if it's not very much, feels like a lot because it's still more than you're giving yourself. You will put this person on a pedestal and overvalue their contribution while crushing yourself. They're just not *that* special. Whether you came into this relationship with low self-esteem or it's been lowered, NC is likely to be needed because taking care of your wellbeing is not your priority. As a result of likely prioritising *their* feelings, needs, wishes and expectations while giving yourself a hard time and acting like you don't matter as much, you're going to end up in considerably more pain. This has a knock-on effect because if you judge yourself on a perspective gained from what you perceive as your screw-ups or flaws, that affects your mindset and behaviour, which affects your choices, which affects who you'll become involved with. NC is a self-esteem builder.

3) **When they're already in a relationship with someone else.** If they're still trying to continue a relationship with you or are at the very least trying to keep you as an option while being with someone else, NC will shut this shadiness down. *Right down.* If you've already had the affair,

you'll find that NC becomes pivotal as it protects you from being drawn back in on the fake promise of them leaving. If you haven't had an affair but they're tapping you up for one, NC will close it down right now and communicate that you're not available. If you thought you were going to have an affair or you fell for them while they were involved with someone else and hoped that they'd leave, NC is very much needed so that you can grieve the loss of your hopes and expectations and more importantly address why you were willing to go down this road.

4) **When mixed messages through engaging is creating more pain.** Although they may have respected your boundaries in the relationship, they're getting mixed messages by a continued 'friendship' or are not accepting that the relationship is over, making it difficult for you (and them) to move on. Equally, if *you're* getting mixed messages or even making up your own interpretation in spite of what they've said or done, NC is imperative for clear messages on both sides. Basically if you're not over them but you're trying to continue being around them, you're actually hurting yourself unnecessarily.

5) **When they're stalking you.** It doesn't matter if they were nice as pie in the relationship – if they're stalking you now that the relationship is over, NC and involving the law are necessary. If you've even been tempted to stalk this person, an enforced time out for you is critical for helping you to regain control of yourself.

6) **When they're abusive.** Trying to be friends or tip-toeing around someone who has already abused you sends mixed messages *plus* it's like giving them a clean slate as they assume that you engaging with them means that their behaviour is acceptable or forgiven, or even that you accept liability for their mistreatment. You don't need to appease an abuser – you need to act with self-preservation and with additional support, you need to distance yourself.

24

7) **When they're a user.** Using is abusing although it may have taken a while to recognise that they've been exploiting a perceived vulnerability in order to gain an advantage. 99% of users will not admit to being a user because it's not how they like to see themselves or they're not going to admit to it, otherwise the advantage ends. Using *feels* like using and losing, and that's all that you need to know. If you feel that you're being taken advantage of, it's because your inner self (that you've likely been ignoring) recognises it.

8) **When there's codependency.** If you don't know where they begin and you end, you've got problems, especially if it feels as if you can't live with or without them, and gaining approval and attention from them is 'necessary' or even 'critical'. This includes when they're addicted to something – for the future wellbeing of you both, it's vital that you separate and take responsibility for your own lives. You also feature here if the feeling that you associate with letting go of this relationship is 'abandonment'.

9) **When you don't truly know the person.** There's a lot of people collecting ex-dates, people they chatted briefly (or even sexted) with online before they disappeared for a time, crushes, extended flirtations and the list goes on – they're people who rent space in their lives despite being almost strangers or greatly exaggerated in their minds. If you're the type of person who can cope with this, that's one thing (you're probably not) but the rot sets in when you have some level of attachment to all of these people and are basically trying to keep them as an option in case one of them spontaneously combusts into being a fairy-tale ending. If you're an option, you're not available.

10) **When you've lost your own respect.** As a result of your involvement, you're doing things that you now or in the future will come to regard as at best embarrassing and at worst humiliating.

11) **When there are boundary issues.** When you or they didn't respect your boundaries in the relationship and are continuing the habit *outside* of it, NC is critical because it removes the opportunity for them to harm you *plus* it allows you to respect your own boundaries in the process, something that isn't going to happen if you continue engaging.

WHERE NOT TO APPLY NC... AT LEAST NOT INITIALLY...

To break off a relationship for the first time.
Unless they're abusive, the first time that you break up, you should let them know that you're ending it. **No Contact comes *after* the breakup and isn't the breakup in its entirety.** If you use NC to break up for the first time for no other reason than that you don't want to have an awkward conversation, this isn't NC; it's *disappearing* – something that's not only cowardly, but can be extremely painful for the person on the receiving end.

The truth is that you wouldn't want it to be done to you and if you were able to find your way *in* to this relationship, you can manage the courtesy of a breakup and an explanation *before* you make your exit because if you don't, that person may end up feeling very rejected and chasing you down for an explanation or even giving themselves an unnecessarily hard time.

If you *are* in an abusive relationship or you suspect that this person may cause you harm, I would highly recommend that you plan your exit carefully and that you speak with a professional including the police, a legal representative, a therapist or support service as well as a trusted friend or family member so that you can make a safe exit. The reason that you can go straight to NC is that abuse negates the need for you to explain and abusive people can be highly manipulative by switching to the charm offensive and/or being very threatening when you try to end things. They may appear calm and then do something destructive or cause you physical harm. Hence a planned exit where you have support to protect you and help you stick to your guns is critical. I talk about this subject in the chapter on *The Get Out Plan.*

To end your marriage.

Cutting contact isn't the way to let someone know that your marriage is over, unless it's an abusive one. Not only do you need to stay in touch for your divorce but it's a pretty nasty way to end a relationship with someone you were prepared to legally bind yourself to! While you can use it for the person who won't respect your boundaries, this is *after* you've told them that the marriage is over and you've already tried the traditional breakup route. Once you've stated that it's over and they show that they don't want to accept it or respect your boundaries, defer to a mediator or legal representative.

Why A Traditional Breakup Isn't Going To Cut It

1. The person who needs to be cut off has an intense need to control you in and out of the relationship. They mistake desire to control you for desire and so when they feel out of control (i.e. when you end things), they will feel consumed by the desire to get you back 'on side'.

2. Even if they appear to initially go along with the breakup, they can actually start looking to get the fringe benefits of a relationship without the commitment or treating you appropriately.

3. If you have a pattern of having slack boundaries and your own mismatched actions and words, your credibility is undermined so they don't take you seriously and believe that you'll 'come round'.

4. They are intent on keeping you as an option should they have a purpose for you at a later date or change their mind – by never removing you as an option, they also never have to admit that they're wrong or have to deal with the fact that they've made mistakes, or even just deal with what should be the natural consequences of their decision; you no longer being available.

5. They often regard you like property – they'd rather you were miserable and an option for them than happy with someone else. They may even think that you moving on to something better would make them look like a mug/asshole, especially if they've been telling lies about you to their friends and family...

6. They have their own major issues with rejection and abandonment – it then becomes like you can't be done until they decide that they're done.

7. You ending it may actually resurrect an old hurt which may trigger anger or even rage, or push them into an intense mode of Future Faking (promising or implying a future, including saying that they'll change in order to get what they want in the present) and Fast Forwarding (trying to speed you back into the relationship using emotional, physical and possibly sexual intensity to distract from and distort the main issues) to convince you to come back.

8. A lack of respect and empathy means that not only do your needs not come into the equation but as a result of not being able to understand your position or the impact of their actions on you, boundaries cannot be respected. Hence a breakup cannot be respected.

9. They know they cannot give you what you want but they like your company, enjoy your friendship or ego stroking, or don't see why you should deny each other the pleasure of sex – they feel OK about things, so they assume that you do or 'should' do too.

10. They may be trapped by their feelings, something that you may

also be experiencing. These can be feelings of anger, rejection or their vision of things, but if it's very intense, a traditional breakup won't pierce their bubble.

Is No Contact Permanent?

NC is as permanent as you want it to be, but the golden rule is that you can only restart or accept contact when you are completely over him/her and have moved on. I suggest making it permanent for someone that has added little or no value to your life and has in fact detracted from it by treating you without love, care, trust and respect. There is no point in keeping contact for ego's sake, as it will mostly be their ego that gets massaged.

At the bare minimum, NC should be enforced for around 3 months but it's likely to be for six months to a year, *especially* if it was a toxic relationship.

If they've disappeared on you before, or you've broken up or have even attempted NC previously, you'll need to take the longest period of time that they've ever disappeared for and *significantly* exceed it. While there isn't a science to it, if the longest you've been NC for is three months, you will likely need to be NC for five to six months at least, but more likely in the nine months to a year region. Of course, it's all about what you *do* with the time because if you use the time well – whether it's one month or three months – if and when they pop back in your life, it won't matter. If you use NC to bide your time for the next instalment of drama and to blame yourself and do other unhealthy stuff, whether it's one month, one year or *ten* years, you will respond to your ex in an unhealthy manner and be right back into the cycle.

It's important to remember that NC is about using this time to address your habits and to build up *your* resources and resilience. If you engage under the premise that they've changed, you're just setting yourself up for a big fall and it exposes an underlying motivation to use NC as a means of attempting to prompt your ex into changing.

Think of NC like giving up smoking – it'll hurt in the short term and you'll be tempted to light up a few times in the first few weeks, but after a while, you feel better than you expected and time is disappearing. You don't give up smoking with a view to maybe lighting up again in a few months' time because that's already showing a lack of commitment to changing your habits. Equally, it's best to embark on NC with the view to moving on, not trying to schedule in when you can next hang out with them.

You're likely to obsess and panic about the fact that you may not hear from them again but if you truly are doing NC for the right reasons and you keep the focus on yourself, you will move on with your life and it won't matter to you whether they get back in touch. And if they do, it won't derail you. It's important to remember that breakups are about ending and changing the nature of a relationship and moving forward. Yes some people do become genuine friends after a breakup but plenty of people *don't* yet do however manage to maintain very destructive connections.

People who are genuine friends after their relationships or who end up being in touch in a non-destructive manner, do so organically. They don't contrive to reconnect; they bump into each other or cross paths while getting on with their respective lives and don't seek to force something for the sake of one or both egos.

When one of your biggest concerns is whether it's permanent, it's a sign that you really need to focus on the process and dealing with your own life *not* theirs. You're still too invested and you need to shuffle around your priorities.

Most people with decent levels of self-esteem think it's odd when the other party wants to be friends straight away. People who need NC applied to them tend to think they can make their own rules and people who need to do NC often worry too much about how they look.

Asking if NC is permanent is like asking if a breakup is permanent.

Yes there's a possibility that one day your paths may cross under better circumstances but we do have to treat our breakups as permanent otherwise we end up in limbo which can expose us to hurt and derail or even stall our lives. Treating breakups as permanent helps the grieving process and keeps you in reality, so that if much further down the line getting back together is revisited, you don't end up making the decision based on bullshit and a mentality driven by failure to process your grief and to recover from disappointment.

NC is recognition of the fact that this relationship is, or was, unhealthy and it may stem from the fact that your other half cannot respect even basic boundaries or that you're not able to act with self-love around them. These are not indicators of a potential friendship and ultimately you need to concern yourself with being a very good friend to *you* instead of worrying about what you're going to do in the future with someone who you don't share a healthy present or past with.

NC isn't about priming yourself to be able to handle someone's assholery in a more 'mature' manner (read: pretending that your needs, expectations and wishes don't matter and ignoring your true feelings) – the mature manner is distance, self-preservation and refusing to accept mistreatment.

Objection! But What About Closure? What if... ?

Part of the reason unhealthy relationships and their even unhealthier breakups drag on long past their sell-by-date is because there is this idea that the other person holds the key to 'closure', this sense of resolution at the end of the relationship and that it's been 'resolved'. This can mean resolving the questions that the relationship may bring up, or attempting to understand the other person, or attempting to understand every last thing that went on in the relationship. In the worst of cases, it's basically like attempting to seek 100% of the answers before feeling that we can put the relationship down. What we don't realise, is that many of us use this idea of seeking closure as a means of avoiding using our own judgement and engaging in decision-making, to avoid this perennial fear of 'making a mistake'.

Closure then becomes wanting to be 100% certain that it wasn't your fault, or that you did everything that *you* could do (which may include taking the blame and the responsibility for the other person's contribution or for the entire relationship). To be 100% sure that ultimately the relationship is unworkable and that they're not going to change into a better person in a better relationship as soon as your back is turned.

If you keep engaging and are still trying to talk the hell out of your relationship because you love to have 'the conversation' and are convinced you need to have a breakup moment of enough magnitude to motivate you to step away, it's because you think it's what you need for closure and you like wondering "What if?"

What if I play doormat a little bit more? Maybe they'll finally see how great I am?
What if I stand by my man/woman?
What if I expect nothing at all? Maybe they won't feel so pressured.
What if I finish it and then they become The Ideal Man/Woman™ for the next person?
Maybe I should have waited a bit longer. We've only broken up 57 times and I've only given umpteen chances, but ya know – maybe I was being a little hasty?

I'm going to say something that you may find difficult to face: **With people that don't know their arses from their elbow, blow hot and cold and won't commit to either being with you or not being with you, you've got to toughen up. Big time.**

What if I play doormat a little bit more? Maybe they'll finally see how great I am? What if I stand by my man/woman?

Yes you could be even more accommodating and try even *harder* to please someone who has no intention of ever realising your greatness, but while you may communicate how much you're 'there' for them, the *other* message communicated is that you have no self-respect, that you have low self-esteem, and that they can get away with mistreating you.

What if I expect nothing at all from them? Maybe they won't feel so pressured.

Every relationship requires expectations. The only reason you're trying to downgrade your expectations is some cack-handed attempt to minimise the amount of disappointment you experience. You expect nothing and they get the very strong message that there are no boundaries and that they're free to do as they like. This isn't happy clappy land. People don't always do the decent thing. It's not like they're going to say "There, there. He/she expects nothing so I'll be nice to them." They'll just have you marked as a soft touch. It's also important to note that often when we go out of our way not to expect anything from people, it's a subconscious way of hoping that they don't expect too much of us, as we're not convinced of our own value and think that if they expect, they may be disappointed. Many people in these situations don't know how to differentiate between expecting what any decent human being should want to give, versus being accused of being needy for effectively breathing and not allowing them to walk all over you.

What if I finish it and then they become The Ideal Man/Woman™ for the next person?

While I can say 'Who cares?', it's obvious that *you* do! It doesn't matter if they're kind to the nice old lady next door or act like Mr/Miss Perfect with the next person, because they're not behaving that way with you, and you actually have no idea whether they're truly being that way in their new relationship either, nor can you judge things based on the honeymoon phase that they may be in currently. You can't hold onto someone in the hope that one day you'll be happy with them. You also can't behave like the equivalent of a squatter or a protestor who won't get off a property – it's only *yourself* that you're imprisoning. Get happy now. It's also important to point out that situations like this expose an incompatibility in values because you've attempted to proceed with this relationship based on who they *are* and that doesn't work for you. If they've found someone who they have compatible values with, even if you don't agree with what those values are, that's their prerogative because you have no right to expect or even demand that they change their values to accommodate you.

Maybe I should have waited a bit longer. We've only broken up 57 times and I've only given umpteen chances, but ya know – maybe I was being a little hasty?

'Conversations' with someone who you've been going nowhere with, who has been using you, sleeping with you when it suits, disappearing, coming back, making promises, breaking promises, abusing you, messing with your mind, unable to commit, withholding their attentions and affections, disrupting the progress of the relationship etc, don't make a blind bit of difference – they just give you a reason to look for that one little eeeny weeny nugget of something to justify an already disproportionate investment and give them a chance, and then they turn around and do the same thing all over again!

One day you wake up and realise that you've spent more time seeking *closure* than you have actually *living* and *enjoying* your relationship.

Wise up, toughen up, smell the coffee and take control of yourself because you cannot control this and the way this relationship is going but you *can* control how YOU are affected by being with him/her, plus you can get closure without them being the one to close the door for you. Why on earth do you need this person to close the door for *your* closure? What you must remember here is that if they were seeking closure themselves, you wouldn't need to *do* NC. It is the fact that they want to leave the proverbial door and their options open that you're in this situation in the first place.

They don't want to explain, they don't want to match actions and words, they don't *want* to provide you with all of the information because then you might tell them to jog on and then you're not an option anymore and they have to face their *own* feelings. You are *not* Siamese twins which means they are not under obligation to provide you with 'double closure'. *You* can close the door and damn well slam it shut when they try to push it back open and *that* is the barometer of how successful NC is:

When they attempt to open the door, there must be no response. The door must be closed, not slightly ajar to hear whatever rinky dinky, bullshit excuse they have. No Contact is a beginning, not an end.

NC enables you to close the door on this relationship even when you *don't* get to have a 'conversation' or a big breakup moment. This time and space that you have to get acquainted with your own perspective and feelings and to reach your *own* resolution because you use NC as an opportunity to grieve, to adjust your perspective, to answer the question of "How did I get here?", to reach a conclusion, and to make a resolution that helps you stand firm behind your original decision to break up and then do NC.

You were in this relationship *too*. The great majority of questions you have can be answered with your own eyes, ears and judgement and so that's another sideline benefit of NC. You gain a huge amount of self-knowledge by trusting yourself to evaluate the situation and to act on your own judgement while getting to know your feelings so that you can build self-awareness.

This is going to be a hugely beneficial period of your life because you will become acquainted with your own feelings, needs, desires and expectations and you will be able to meet these better but also find a relationship that is more befitting of you by learning from the insights gained. You do not need *their* help in order to do this.

Objection! What If They Get In Touch?

Many people who embark on NC make the mistake of expending a lot of brainpower thinking about when and if their ex will get in touch and then pondering their possible response. This is more energy than this deserves and you are still making this person the focal point of your life despite the fact that they're technically no longer in it. Accept that it's possible that they're going to attempt to make contact but also stay focused on your own needs. If you worry about whether they're going to make contact and how you're going to fall off the wagon when they do, it's like praying to break NC and end up in pain, which is what you don't want. Worry is like a goldfish – it doesn't know when it's full so you will overfeed it. Stop overfeeding it.

Just because they may attempt to make contact doesn't mean that you have to give him/her what they want.

Just because they call/email/text, doesn't mean that you have to answer or reply.

Just because they turn up on your doorstep, doesn't mean that you can't turn them away.

You can end up believing that people who are worthy of being dated and in relationships and worthy of love are the type of people who get the object of their previous affections coming back to them, or at least trying to. The reality is that if the person you cut it off with believes any of the following, they won't be in touch. Yet.

- That the same conditions to which they have become used to no longer exist.
- That making contact might restart a cycle of something that they don't wish to restart, for example, you wondering why they haven't left their wife/when they're going to change/why they don't yet understand how they have hurt you.

- That they have found someone who allows them to do as they please.
- That they pissed you off so much the last time they spoke with you that they believe that there will be serious negative consequences.

In fact, there could be umpteen reasons why someone hasn't, or won't get in touch with you, but it's a bit like wondering how long a piece of string is… Always remember that if they get in touch, it's not because you're destined to be together in love's young dream. Making contact is their way of testing to see if the door is still open. Your job is to communicate through your actions (lack of response) that it is closed.

Objection! But What About When The Unexpected Happens?

When people contemplate NC, they worry about the possibility of bumping into their ex or picking up a call from an unlisted number and finding their ex on the other end – neither of these things mean that NC has been broken. Yes NC is about minimising, and where possible eliminating, the possibility for your ex to contact you (or you them) but you cannot control the uncontrollable. This is about cutting off *your* end of things and not engaging unnecessarily.

Unexpected things will happen or sometimes contact is unavoidable (you have children together, work together or have some paperwork to finalise) but you can do all of these things without *engaging*.

You can drop your children off or address an issue about school without sleeping together or doing round #250 of the *Why couldn't you give me what I wanted?* discussion. You can be professional and civil *without* having to do any of the things that you used to do in your relationship and you can finalise paperwork or even discuss an issue about your property without engaging beyond this.

Incidentally, you may both like the same places but take the high road, and for now, until you're in a stronger place, **don't go to places where you're likely to meet**. You're just creating pain for yourself and potentially creating drama. It might be 'your bar' but you need 'your life' and 'your sanity' more than you need 'that bar'.

What *does* help is preparing for the unexpected and I talk about these subjects throughout the book because with even the best will in the world, you could block contact and not make any and then randomly bump into your ex in the supermarket and be caught off guard. The key is not to take the unexpected as some sort of sign that you're supposed to engage or even drop your pants.

Objection! But What About When We Didn't Have A Relationship?

You would be amazed at how many people find themselves in a situation of having to 'break up' with someone they haven't *actually* had a full-on relationship with. Aside from the obvious booty call and Friends With Benefits situations, there are some very common examples of situations that require NC even though they're not 'relationships'.

- You fancied this person like crazy, professed your feelings, they turned you down but have then persisted in flirting with you and trying to keep you close for an ego stroke.
- You realised they were married so you backed away but they keep pursuing you while at the same time reminding you about how they're married and working on their marriage when you ask what the hell is going on.
- You're unable to continue what was previously a genuine friendship because of your romantic feelings that you'd hoped

would have gone away by now.

- After being crazy about a 'friend' for ages, you've finally realised that you're not going to be more than friends and that you don't actually want to be friends because they're not actually friendship material and you only called them your friend to legitimise hanging around them.

- They flirt and spend lots of time around you, and even appear to act a bit jealous when you say you've been on a date, but when you push them on what's going on between you both, they claim that you've 'misunderstood' him/her. Note, you haven't misunderstood a damn thing other than thinking that they want to do anything beyond messing with your mind and your feelings.

- You chatted with him/her on a dating site, they don't seem to want to take things anywhere but they like emailing you for an ego stroke and you've found it difficult to detach.

- You met ages ago, you gave them your number, and since then they call/email/text but it never goes beyond this. They may have disappeared after you broached the subject of what was going on between you and it's all very ambiguous or even game-like.

- You've had a crush on them and they didn't reciprocate and you're finding it difficult to recover from what feels like a rejection.

These are only some examples and the reason you'll want and need to cut contact is because you've found yourself becoming emotionally invested, chasing them for attention and validation, wondering if you've done something wrong, or wondering what you need to do to progress things beyond *their* terms.

You may think that this is excessive due to it seeming like you're breaking up without a relationship. No Contact is just as applicable here because, for the sake of your sanity and to protect you from being drawn into any more illusions, the distance created will allow you to breathe and move on to people who are actually available to you.

If you have a tendency to lose yourself in the fantasy, NC is critical for bringing you back to earth.

Trust me, I've heard so many tales of how people have lost months and years of their lives waiting around for someone who has no intention of becoming anything more, and all because they believe that there's something going on, or that at some point, their feelings are going to be reciprocated. It's only through putting distance between them that they suddenly realise that there was nothing going on and they've been emotionally investing in a fantasy when they actually want to be loved in reality.

This period of NC is for reconciling any illusions you've been under with reality. Distancing yourself from this person will not only neutralise the effect of your interest/their actions but it will also enable you to find happiness with both of your feet on the ground and your self-esteem in tow.

Can't We Just Be Friends?

It's not long after the words have been uttered that render your relationship over, that some form of request for friendship will be made. It's almost as if we have all received some sort of relationship training that makes people the world over trot out the words as a form of consolation that hopefully dilutes the strained discussion and makes you look a better person in their eyes. It's like "Hey. I know I'm done screwing with you, but what the hell? Let's be friends because I'll feel like less of a prick if you say yes..."

Truth be told, most people don't really mean it when they say that they want to stay friends. It's just the polite thing to say.

Hell I've said it to almost all of my exes and lo and behold, I don't keep in touch with any of them and I haven't sought to add them as a friend on Facebook! Not only is it very difficult to go from holding hands to platonic friends but you don't do it as a follow-on from a breakup. In order to break up, there needs to be a BREAK. There needs to be distance and time to allow each person to heal and move on. This time can't be spent playing best mates with one of you acting like you feel less than you do.

The only people that can be friends after having a relationship are those that feel nothing romantically for each other, are no longer emotionally invested, and there has been a healthy distance between you to allow you both to move on. This is not you. At least not yet. You might *think* you're ready, but if you stay friends right now, it's because you want to be validated, you want to keep an eye on them, and you're secretly hoping that they'll POOF! turn into the perfect partner and all of your previous troubles will be washed away.

Friendship is a mutual relationship between friends.

If it's not mutual, you're not friends. If you have an ulterior motive, you're not friends. If you're not over them yet, you're not friends. If it's about your ego, you're not friends. If it would bother you if they were involved with someone else, you're not friends. If you're keeping yourself as an option, you're definitely not friends. If this whole friendship thing is a way to avoid doing right by yourself, that's laziness and it's not a healthy friendship. If you don't think that a friendship will be there if you have space, you're not friends and you're afraid that if you don't please this person now and cater to their ego, that you will 'miss out' and then someone else will get a better version of this person in a better relationship. Enough.

I'm not suggesting that you can't ever be friends but make up your mind about what you're doing here because there are millions of people out there kicking themselves for allowing friendship to be used as an 'open sesame' to be treated like a doormat. Take the break, do the work on yourself and if a friendship is going to happen between you, it will happen organically and be a genuine friendship. If a few months go by and you're still trying to pursue a friendship, it's a sign that you're not ready yet because they're still a priority. If this relationship was abusive in any way though, it's time to call curtains on it and let it go. You need clean, healthy relationships and you don't need to collect trophies of all of your exes. If you're really intending to move on, you have to think about what place your ex really has in your life. You've both had your time. Whatever it was meant to be, it's been. Let it be.

****

There are other aspects of your life where you will find that while you can't cut contact completely, for instance with family, a friend, the mother/father of your child etc, you can do something that you should be doing anyway, which is teach them how to treat you and what they can expect from you moving forward by having and enforcing boundaries. I cover some of this in the book because toxic and difficult relationships don't always come in standard breakup flavour.

Whether you're in or out of a relationship or feeling as if the walls are closing in due to everyone taking advantage of you, the foundations of NC are incredibly empowering if you follow through and believe in yourself. It's important when embarking not only on NC but on moving forward with your life and treating yourself with love, care, trust and respect even where others fail to, that you plan for success not failure. Believe that you can close the door on this painful relationship so you can open the door to a better future.

40 SIGNS THAT NC IS A NECESSITY

Over the years of helping people to evaluate their situation and recognise when No Contact is needed, I've come to recognise the very typical feelings and situations that are being dealt with. If you agree with just *one* of these statements, it's highly likely that you need NC. If you agree with any of these statements or even a number of them and have *previously* tried to end this relationship, or are even trying to be their 'friend' as a means of auditioning for the relationship hot seat, or you're trying to negotiate a reconciliation, are sleeping with them, or are finding it difficult to cope with the rejection, cutting contact is imperative.

1. *This is one-sided. My feelings are not reciprocated but I am still hanging around.*

2. *This relationship is conducted on their terms. If I attempt things my way, I'm met with objections, stonewalling, silence, disappearing or hostility.*

3. *I feel as if I'm losing my mind in this relationship. In fact, other areas of my life have suffered greatly as well.*

4. *I've tried to break up but they just won't listen, or I keep going back.*

5. *I've asked them to give me some space – they persist in attempting to contact me despite repeated warnings to stop.*

6. *I'm considering taking out a restraining order. Another person might describe what they're doing as stalking.*

7. *They blow hot when I tell them that it's over or that things are not*

working, and then gradually, or even rapidly ease down to lukewarm or even cold.

8. There's an absence of love, care, trust and respect. I've had my trust breached.

9. I'm engaging in at best, embarrassing and at worst, humiliating behaviour.

10. I feel as if I've been rejected several or many times but I keep going back.

11. It feels as if I have a compulsion/addiction to this person and I keep returning to the relationship even though I consistently end up disappointed.

12. I have little or no boundaries in the relationship and our dynamic relies on this. If I had more boundaries they wouldn't be around.

13. They're a Future Faker, faking a future with me to get what they need in the present and I've been caught out by their fakery on a number of occasions.

14. I regard this person as an assclown, someone who treats me with little or no regard and is using me to serve their own needs.

15. They are devoid of empathy and do not care about the impact of their actions or words on me. In fact, they're actually a diagnosed narcissist/sociopath/ psychopath.

16. They're not a diagnosed narcissist but they have behaved in ways such as devaluing and discarding me after intense pursuit and interest, having a harem, turning friends and family against me, and having delusions of grandeur that is more than enough to leave me highly concerned about continuing my involvement.

17. I am afraid of this person. They've threatened to harm me/loved ones/ possessions.

18. I've experienced verbal, mental, sexual, physical abuse.

19. I have totally forgotten who I am, my values, my boundaries, what my needs are, my hobbies, family, friends etc. I've become isolated by this relationship.

20. We dated for a relatively short period of time but I've been very affected

by their actions/our involvement ending.

21. *They play the victim and I constantly battle with guilt even though I haven't done what I'm being accused of.*

22. *We've broken up several times.*

23. *We've broken up at least once before for similar reasons.*

24. *They promised that things would change after the last breakup but it's gone back to normal. (They may even have done this several times.)*

25. *When we've been broken up before, they kept trying to sleep with me.*

26. *If someone else were describing this 'relationship' they 'might' call it a booty call or even say it's not a relationship.*

27. *They're trying to continue seeing me even though they're seeing someone else.*

28. *I used to be the girlfriend/boyfriend and now I'm the Other Woman/Man.*

29. *They're attached/married, have promised they'd leave several times, but haven't, but aren't prepared to end this.*

30. *We work together and I'm finding it difficult to establish a professional footing, to fend off their advances or to cope with my hurt.*

31. *They've told me that they don't want a relationship or that they're not interested, or even that they're **never** going to want a relationship but I won't accept it.*

32. *They've actually said to me that I should cut them off for my own sake.*

33. *We're separated/divorced but they're still trying to control me and even think they're entitled to sleep with me or disrupt my life via our children.*

34. *I want to move on but I don't know how to.*

35. *I have contemplated ending my life or have even tried to because of my struggles to overcome this relationship.*

36. *I've been seriously contemplating taking revenge (or already have). In fact, they've taken out a restraining order/threatened to.*

37. *I'm essentially stalking this person on/offline. I'm all over their Facebook page/driving past their home/secretly accessing their email/trespassing on their property etc.*

38. *One or both of us are dealing with dependency on a substance or*

compulsive behaviour, making ours a very codependent relationship.

39. *I feel guilty about ending our involvement and worry that they're going to do something to themselves if I don't remain in contact with them but we cannot have a relationship either.*

40. *Our involvement falls into the fantasy relationship category where it was a crush/virtual (primarily online/texting) relationship and I'm very attached to them and it's wreaking havoc on my life.*

I've dealt with people who actually agree with almost all of these statements for *one* relationship. Code red alert! If you've acclimatised to high-level drama and what is actually severe levels of stress in your life, you are *normalising poor relationship behaviour* that in some cases may be dangerous or even life threatening. You might be saying to yourself that you can 'handle it' or believe that you know better. You don't. Don't let the first time that you take seriously how toxic this relationship is be when you've destroyed your sense of self, or even worse, when your life is in danger.

The above situations and feelings are not what love looks like – it's a list of *pain, danger* and *abuse*. While No Contact may seem like a hardcore act of self-preservation to undertake, it will take you *far* longer to get over this relationship *without* it, than it would have done if you'd slammed the breaks on yourself and committed to the process of loving and living with your self-esteem in tow.

THE PRACTICALITIES

HOW TO DO NC

No Contact involves taking control of your end of the communication channels and removing or minimising the opportunities for contact to be made or received. This not only protects you from disruption by the other party, but it also protects you from making contact in the heat of the moment that you will ultimately go on to regret. Taking preventative measures *now* means that you will also hopefully need to go to a considerable effort to break contact should the inclination grab you, which will hopefully help you to think carefully before you act.

Remember, you need to start regarding the lines of communication as *triggers* and *cues* that you have *responses* to.

They call, you tend to pick up, but you also pick up because you have an emotional response tied to this hope that they might have changed. They text and no matter how ridiculous the content, you feel compelled to reply and part of this is due to the thoughts and fears attached to the perceived consequences of *not* replying, with little regard for the *actual* consequences of replying. By limiting or even removing some of the communication channels, you get to adapt your responses while getting a clearer perspective due to having the space to do so. Whilst you can adapt it a little (see later in the book if you're working together, have kids etc), the suggestions that I make in this chapter are what I highly recommend for starting and maintaining No Contact. From whether to let them know that you're going NC, to dealing with Columboing on Facebook, to how to deal with pesky emails and even those worries about the homemade porno, I've got you covered.

Should You Notify Your Ex That You're Going NC?

Many people who familiarise themselves with what NC involves, very quickly become paralysed by the question of whether they should let their ex know that they're cutting contact.

Why do we want to give them a heads up? Partly because we think that if someone just 'disappeared' on us that we'd be devastated so we don't want to do it to them, and yes, it's also partly due to seeking validation and hoping that pre-warning them may prompt a change of mind and attitude. Aside from the fact that NC isn't the same as disappearing and that you're also not the same person anyway, it's also important to remember that NC is the action part of setting new boundaries, so just like you've had to figure out what is going on even when it's not being spelled out, they do too.

This is one of those situations where you have to use this opportunity to evaluate and process information that you hold on the situation to make a decision that has an overall benefit instead of catering to a short-term or even shortsighted need to cater to your ego or even to theirs.

Once you start NC, it's pointless, if not somewhat childish, to keep saying to the person, "I'm ignoring you" because if you're genuinely doing NC, your actions do all of the talking that's needed. So if you're going to let them know that you're doing NC, do it *before* you start or very soon after (within the first week). After that, leave it alone.

WHAT TO CONSIDER BEFORE NOTIFYING

- Examine your motives for wanting to let them know, especially if you're already broken up. If a part of you is letting them know in the hope that they will change or say something to throw you off your NC course, I would take stock of your situation and ensure that you are behind your decision and validating it with specific reasons for why you're cutting contact.

- If you've been attempting to be friends and it's not working for you but there isn't anything particularly shady happening from their end, saying that you're taking time out and won't be in touch is understandable.

- Be clear. If you're wishy-washy or even dropping hints, you will give out mixed messages which will suggest to the other party that you might want to hear from them. Tell them that *you* will be in touch when you're ready to talk and to leave you alone until then.

- If you've previously attempted to cut contact and have let them know, *don't* let them know this time. It's a credibility issue and you won't be taken seriously even if you feel like you're so much more serious 'this time around'.

- If this relationship was in any way abusive, don't pre-warn them as it may open you up to further abuse.

THE MESSAGE

If you do let them know and you feel compelled to tell them why, do so by phone (as in using your voice not text) or if you really cannot do this, via email or letter. If you feel in control, face-to-face may be an option. The phone is your litmus test though of how much you really need to let them know, because if you would rather, for instance, send a *text message*, you're not really *that* bothered about letting them know – you're just ticking a box that relieves your conscience and yes, possibly even looking for attention. You're also trying to take the easy route that doesn't leave you as 'vulnerable' but if you're that concerned about protecting your vulnerabilities, not sending a message at all would be the better option.

- **Stick to three key points.** Anything else is overkill and heading into Yet Another Big Discussion or Yet Another Opportunity To Tell Them All About Themselves. Bearing in mind that this isn't a democratic decision and you don't need their validation, *one* reason is enough.

- **Keep it short.** Don't send an essay or even a novel.

- **Don't be mean,** as in saying things that are dishonest and disrespectful, or honest but still disrespectful. Meanness (especially written stuff) may give you a reason to feel guilty when you've calmed down plus it tends to trigger the need to apologise, which you might then use to invalidate what is actually a good decision to cut contact.

- **Make the reasons ultimately about you.** "It doesn't work for me to continue things in the way that we have been. I need as much time as it takes for me to move past this" is reason enough as is, "When _____ , _____ and _____ happened, I felt _____ and realised _____." Obviously if you say stuff like you're "You're an asshole" it makes it all about them or if you say, "I'm going NC because you won't change…" it's an invitation for certain types of people to jump on the Future Faking roundabout. If they say something, "But what about my feelings?" or "What about what I want?", it's important to realise that it's not your job to babysit their feelings because what you're doing now is what *you* need and you've already given over more than enough time and energy catering to what *they* need.

- **Don't make it a declaration of your feelings.** It will be a massive ego stroke in the wrong hands. One of the things that you will learn in this book is that a person doesn't have to be around you 24:7 or even at all, if they feel super-secure in the knowledge that you're crazy about them and your whole life is going belly up. Don't feed their ego.

- **If they reply, don't respond.** It sort of goes against the whole you're going NC thing and immediately drags you back into discussion and undermines your credibility. If you can't contain your responding finger and it's going to be your one and only response, five simple words are more than enough – my mind is made up.

Remember, you've had a whole relationship and a breakup so even though you might be feeling like you need to 'enlighten' them, they *do* have an idea of why your relationship didn't work even if they're protesting otherwise or even playing the innocent. The harder that you try to convince them, the more that it looks like it's you that you're trying to convince.

Phone Communication

You need to limit the ability for this person to reach you on any of your phones – home, cell/mobile, work, Skype and similar – and you of course need to ensure that you don't reach out or respond via any of these means. If they call from an undisclosed number or they catch you off guard at the office, just get off the phone as quickly as possible. Hang up even. This section also covers texting, the laziest of communications that has kept many a shady relationship/'connection' alive.

You know when you get those texts saying stuff like "Hope you're well...?" or "Talking to me yet?" or "I miss our talks" and other such guff, they're fishing texts.

Besides being incredibly lazy means of reaching out to you and effectively crumbs of attention and communication, texts certainly don't rank highly on showing even a moderate level of care and if you overvalue them, they create faux intimacy. The trouble with texts is that they can give the impression that you're on someone's mind, while being very open to interpretation as they tend to be read in the way that you think that they were written, not how they actually were.

1. Evaluate your phone habits. This is a good time to think about the way that you use your phone because if you've become a slave to it and are jumping out of your skin each time it calls or you seem to spend your whole life tapping out messages and checking to see if your voicemail is broken, or are prone to taking calls and responding to messages at all sorts of hours, this cannot continue if you want to be successful at NC and you also want to have a life and a decent nights sleep. New habits to practice may include:

❖ Turning off your phone after a certain time.

❖ Only checking your phone a few times a day, such as when you get into work, lunch time, mid-afternoon, after work, before you wind down for the evening.

❖ If you tend to spend most of your time on your phone surfing while travelling, it may be beneficial to take something to read or limit the amount of time you spend surfing.

❖ Returning calls after, for example, 9 pm the following day is good practice. In this day and age, most people know that if it's a genuine emergency, they can call your landline.

❖ Check to see if your phone has a 'Do Not Disturb' setting. Mine comes on at 10 pm because I was being driven batty by notifications from apps that seem to ignore that you've turned off sound notifications.

2. Consider turning off your text plan. It's becoming increasingly common for people to turn off their text plans. Not only does it remove temptation but it can work wonders for making an effort with friends and family. It's easy to fall into the trap of thinking, "But what if they're trying to reunite with me but they're unable to text?" and aside from the fact that your thoughts don't need to be on a reunion right now, if there's genuine intention with matching actions to back it up, it won't happen in a text…

3. Delete their number as soon as possible. If you're going to keep it, do so for no more than three months and that's *only* so that you know it's him/her if they decide to call/text and you'll know not to answer. Otherwise wipe out all information you have on them as soon as possible, especially because you'll hopefully have to go to some effort to retrieve it.

4. Change their name in your phone or the ringtone. Put a nickname that will trigger a mental reminder to stick to NC or go for a song that epitomises your situation. The song of choice for many readers has been Jar of Hearts by Christina Perri.

5. Is it a block or change number situation? If their inability to respect your boundaries is pretty serious, check with your network provider about blocking their number or, you may need to consider changing yours. If you do change your number, only disclose it to those close to you and request that nobody passes on your number under any circumstance. The chief objection to changing numbers – aside from the inconvenience – is this sense of not wanting to give this person 'power' over you, but guess what? When someone is wreaking havoc with your head and your life by being a nuisance, that's just another form of that person having 'power' through disruption. There comes a point when you have to decide whether you want to open yourself to the possibility of hearing from them or whether you want this to end. What this person is doing *isn't* flattering and they may actually be getting off on this idea that due to being a nuisance, you're being affected. They're able to control you because it may be disruptive to your health as well as your relationships.

❖ If changing your number seems drastic, put your mobile/cell on voicemail and get a temporary pay-as-you-go phone which only a limited number of people are made aware of.

6. Do check the laws in your country. In the UK it is an offence to continue to call or send unwanted messages to someone more than twice, especially after you've requested that they stop or told them not to contact you in the first place. If you are receiving nuisance calls and messages or the tone has become threatening, do seek advice from the police and make sure that you keep a record of calls and texts. Let's not forget that it's also an offence in most countries to stalk and harass.

- ❖ If they're a work colleague and are using their company phone to badger you, they may actually be breaching the company's terms and conditions.
- ❖ A word of caution – be careful of engaging after reporting to the police because it can undermine your case no matter what your intentions were.

7. Screen. Let calls go to voicemail, especially if you don't recognise the number. This is especially the case for pesky, shameless exes who will borrow people's phones and go to great lengths to bust your boundaries.

8. Delete voicemails and texts (excluding anything threatening obviously). Some people delete messages without listening and some delete after listening. Either way delete because it prevents replaying. It's important to consider *why* you're listening. For validation? Hope that they've 'changed'? This will undermine your NC efforts so be careful. You are also likely to find that listening to voicemails from somebody who has already caused you pain is a painful disruption you can do without. If you're prone to nostalgia, it may be time to do a big delete on your texts or investigate the possibility of archiving.

- ❖ iPhones are a pain in the bum for doing full clean deletes. It may be worthwhile taking it to the store where you purchased or contacting your network provider for suggestions.

9. Make yourself invisible on Skype and similar services. Or make it even easier for yourself and remove them so that they can't message you.

Or just don't log on if you don't need to. If you don't do any of these, the one thing I would do is change the preferences on your computer so that you're not automatically logged into Skype each time you shut down and restart.

Email

It's best to neutralise, or at the very least limit, the opportunity for email because even outside of NC it creates a great deal of anxiety for people due to many of us feeling harassed by the 'ping' and burdened with our own expectation that we 'must' respond to all emails, or even that we must respond *immediately*. There are several key things that can keep you out of a lot of trouble with email:

1. Check with your ISP/email provider about blocking and filter options. Filters automatically select and redirect mail to a folder or trash based on the parameters you've specified which can include a specific email address or even keywords.

2. Go invisible or turn off the chat function. If you're on the same type of email (e.g. Gmail, Hotmail), make sure that it shows you as invisible when you log in and disable the chat function (if applicable) if you think that they're likely to message you on it.

3. Steer clear of conflict on company email. I talk about this further in the chapter on working together, but do avoid responding on company email, especially if it results in you telling them all about themselves or even pouring out your feelings. I've seen too many instances of these being used against the person and *them* being made to look like *they're* the one harassing. Don't let the first time that you take this seriously be when you're sitting in HR and your job/reputation is at threat. Remember that the less that you respond, the bigger the hole that they dig for themselves.

4. Stop requests. If you decide to reply to their email to request that they stop contacting you, you only need to send *one* email and after that it's ignore and delete or look at implementing #1 if possible as this would eradicate the issue altogether. Don't go into too much detail and just ask them not to send any further emails. Say that this is the last time you'll be responding (and mean it because they may email again to test you). You can add (if you feel that it warrants it) that should you receive any further emails, you will pass them to HR, the police etc, but again, don't go saying this if you're 1) not going to follow through or 2) it's not necessarily warranted. Sometimes all that's needed is, "When I said I needed space, I meant it. Thanks for reaching out but if you send any more, I won't be reading or responding. Please respect my need for space and privacy at this time."

5. Don't read into joke emails. You may have been included as part of a group and ultimately the email doesn't warrant a reply or your energy. A reply isn't expected (or at least it shouldn't be) and remember that you may have been thoughtlessly added or added with a view to prompting you out of your silence, which is just basically getting you to do the legwork. Leave it be.

6. Turn off sound notifications. After at one point feeling like a slave to my phone, I no longer get a sound notification and have to specifically go into my mail to get new mail through. I also tend to close down my email for chunks of time because the sound (if the volume is on) is a distraction. Of course the chief reason for turning off the sound is if you've tended to be a heavy emailer with this person or have become nervous of hearing from them, and the sound may cause unnecessary anxiety.

7. Remember that abuse is never acceptable. It's actually very intimidating to receive a hostile or even threatening email and no one has the right to bully you and use their way with words to dig at you.

Ultimately they're only digging a hole for themselves so print off anything that crosses the line (make sure that the date, time and email address is visible on the printout) and then delete – don't forget to delete in your trash too. Or archive if you know that you won't be tempted to keep rereading it. You may want to have a second copy kept separately just in case.

Facebook

Whether you use Facebook or not, or you use it a little or a lot, do not skip over this section, because Facebook can end up becoming your Achilles heel when you get into the habit of passively but possibly very persistently keeping tabs on your ex or torturing yourself over what they're up to. Even people who aren't on Facebook can get sucked into the pastime of 'rifling' if their ex's page is 'public'!

Due to social networking being such an easy means of prying without leaving a trace, it's important to set some personal boundaries and remove temptation and distractions because if you don't, you could find yourself very mentally, emotionally and even physically affected – I hear from people who lose entire days in the 'Facebook Vortex'. It is all too easy to put two and two together and make forty, to engage in comparison, to turn the pressing of 'like' into a whole week's worth of drama and to basically open yourself up to pain.

Facebook is Kryptonite for people with wobbly self-esteem and super-busy imaginations.

Now I use Facebook and enjoy it to a degree, but Facebook knows its place in my life because *I* know its place in my life. It's not the oracle nor the key to life; it is a social networking website not a person, and it's largely based on people projecting images of themselves which are not always accurate.

Many readers who've struggled with NC have found it a lot easier after self-imposed bans. Why? Because *you* can get on with your life and you also don't have to deal with your ex using Facebook whether it's directly or through friends to poke around in your life and cause problems.

It's not real life and the connections on there are not equivalent to having a great 'connection' in reality unless a true, mutual relationship, romantic or otherwise, exists. For your own inner peace, it is important to be honest about whether Facebook has the potential to affect you or already is, and carefully consider how you're going to limit its impact.

1. Evaluate whether you need to step away from it until you're in a better headspace. If you tend to get bothered or even upset by what people post, or you judge yourself based on how you feel you're not measuring up, it would be best to take a Facebook break until you're feeling more at peace within yourself. It's not worth keeping up appearances on a website at the expense of your happiness, so use the time off to get a better perspective.

2. If checking Facebook feels compulsive, it's time to deactivate. When hours or even days are slipping through your fingers as you obsessively keep an eye on what they (or their friends) are posting, deactivating your account until you've regained self-control is strongly recommended. I would also consider deactivating if you and your ex are heavy users and it has already been a source of drama between you both. You will not lose any of your information and if and when you're ready, you can resume as if you never left but hopefully with healthier usage habits.

3. Limit the amount of time that you spend on Facebook. I know people who are on there all day long. Seriously, it's not good for you, breakup or not. Limit it to checking three times a day for 5-10 minutes at a time so that you don't end up having the day sucked into a Facebook vacuum. This isn't just so that you don't end up torturing yourself over updates that pop up (there's a remedy for that – see #4 and #5) but it's also because if you're feeling quite raw, reading updates from people who may be exaggerating their own lives or sharing joys that you'd hoped to be experiencing but aren't, will deflate you.

4. Hide their profile from your news feed. If you can handle Facebook but just need to tune out your ex, you can hide their profile as well as those of mutual friends who you haven't gotten around to defriending yet. At the time of publication (you know Facebook likes screwing around with the settings and interface), you can do this by clicking on the top right of their update in your newsfeed or you can go to their timeline and ensure that you're not subscribed to their updates.

5. If they didn't treat you well in the relationship and/or have behaved in ways that bust your boundaries post breakup, *defriend.* A lot less people would experience considerably less angst if they stopped with the faux friendships and feeding this anxiety about virtual social standing. Defriend! They're not your friend! They also don't know about it until they attempt to view your profile so it's not as if they get notified. The true reason why there is so much angst about defriending during NC is because it is the end of *your* access to them and severs a tie, but that's what the whole idea of NC is.

6. Update your privacy settings and ensure that it's either set to 'friends' (ideal) or 'friends of friends'. Do keep in mind that if you defriend your ex but remain connected to mutual friends, they may be able to see what you post, particularly if that friend 'likes' or comments on it.

7. Be careful with the content of your status updates. Posting statuses that can be perceived as you sending a veiled message to your ex or mutual friends that you're connected with just fan the tension flames. I would also avoid posting statuses that give the impression that your life is falling apart without your ex, that you're an 'angry person' or even that you're going off the rails. You're inadvertently stroking their ego and possibly even giving them the impression that they're 'justified' in shady behaviour. Think reputation management.

8. Curtail your snooping. Don't open yourself up to hurt by doing the online equivalent of rifling through their photo collection or doing an investigation of every person they're connected with. If you do snoop, don't confront them because you'll end up looking like you're a stalker or at the very least clearly not NC and very invested in them. You can guarantee that a confrontation isn't going to go down well no matter what your intentions. They'll likely have some wishy-washy excuse for it, you'll likely be blocked or defriended (though that might be for the best really) and you may become the subject of gossip amongst your 'mutual friends'. You're supposed to be NC so that includes curtailing your private investigator activities.

9. If you block your ex, make sure that it's what you intended because it's a bit of a palaver to unblock/re-block. Blocking is what you do when the person keeps messaging you even after you've defriended them and you basically want to be as invisible as possible to them. Or change your settings so that only people who you're friends with can message you. Don't get into the whole 'rage blocking' or 'nostalgia induced unblocking' and then panicking cycle because there's a time lag for unblocking (depending on how often you've done it), plus should you change your mind and decide to re-block, there's also at least a 48-hour delay for that too.

10. No 'liking', commenting and responding. If you decide to remain 'friends' on Facebook, you *still* have to do NC. In olden times, your sources of anxiety were limited, whereas now you have too many options for worrying about how you 'look' or what they might be thinking that you're thinking about them. Spare yourself the headache and hide their updates as per #4 and don't respond to anything no matter how innocuous you think it may be. It's not. I've seen people freak out over a clicked like – to think that this wasn't even part of our lives a decade ago and we're so affected by it is quite scary! Remember that due to the ambiguity and sometimes Wild Wild West nature of the internet, clicking on their stuff will send mixed messages that may give this person the impression that it's OK to reach out to you.

11. Change your profile picture if both of you are in it.

12. Rip off the Band-Aid that is changing your relationship status. Not everyone sees or even notices the change and it's got to happen some time.

Twitter

I don't hear as many complaints about Twitter issues and NC as I do about Facebook but when I do hear stories, they're always featuring heavyweight drama because there's something about Twitter and it being about more than just your own circle of friends (who you might normally restrain yourself around), that seems to inspire people to get their drama on through a torrent of 140 character messages.

You will also find that if you're social media savvy and your ex isn't, but they want to keep tabs on you, they'll suddenly develop an interest in Twitter to find ways to stir up trouble so that you'll engage with them. This may include going through your followers and messaging them, reading into innocent tweets, or accusing you of stuff off the back of your updates.

I like social media but it's not worth having your ex on your back, and due to the stream of consciousness feel of Twitter, it's all too easy to sound off and think that it's not going to be seen when it might be. It's not about being fake but it is about considering whether playing out your relationship drama or even a new romance on Twitter is really worth drawing your ex into your life.

1. Don't talk about them on Twitter. The easiest way to minimise aggravation from your ex about your Twitter updates is to ensure that you don't feed the drama. While somebody who wants to misconstrue stuff will latch on to anything and everything to engage with you, make your own life easier by not talking about them (even when you think it's been cleverly disguised) on Twitter. Some people get off on this kind of attention and what you also need to know is that even if your ex doesn't respond to what you post about them, it doesn't mean that they're not reading it and thinking, "Yep, they still want me."

2. No fights. If they're on Twitter too, resist the urge to get drawn into a Twitter spat with them or their mutual friends, or even their current partner. It all ends up looking a bit Jerry Springer/Maury/Jeremy Kyle. Unless that's the look you're going for, bite your Twitter tongue.

3. Consider protecting your updates. If they're harassing you, whether it's on or off Twitter, protecting your updates until things have calmed down may give you some breathing space. Do also keep a screengrab of any offensive tweets (they may delete them after they've got a reaction or when they realise that they're over the line).

4. Don't read their feed. Spare yourself the drama. I would also avoid reading their mentions.

5. There is a block function. This only stops their tweets showing in your feed and any @ replies from showing in your mentions but it doesn't mean that they won't read your updates (they just need to log out if your page is public) nor does it mean that they can't or won't tweet about you.

LinkedIn

The professional networking site gets a mention here for one particular reason: if you read your ex's profile or vice versa, they (or you) will know about it because the site lets each user know who has been viewing their profile, something that many people don't know until they're found out or it notifies them about their ex checking up on them.

I've listened to so many people asking, "I don't understand! Why were they looking at my profile when they don't want to have a relationship with me/give me what I want?" So I know that these notifications can be a great source of angst. Spare yourself and simply don't look and if you discover that they're looking, don't read anything into it. It's curiosity, a quick fix, but it doesn't mean that they've changed or that they want to get back together. It's just LinkedIn.

Most people (yes you and me included) have checked up on somebody from their past when they thought that they could do it without being found out. It's human nature and what a lot of social networking is about. If you make this person looking at your profile into a big deal, you may fall into the trap of making contact, only to end up disappointed all over again. They may know that you get notified and are hoping that you'll do their dirty work and reach out and basically provide confirmation that you're still interested. Don't go there.

Dating Sites, Alumni Sites, Forums, Blogs etc

Over the years I've corresponded with many readers who could probably give the FBI/MI5/CIA a damn good run for their money with their investigative skills. Many of these people believed that they were NC but actually, they weren't because they were giving themselves a false sense of control by monitoring the movements of their exes or even their new partners. Now I'm not suggesting that you don't continue to use websites that you would normally frequent. What I *am* saying is that signing up to, or visiting sites where you know that your ex is a member/user, because they provide a means of you getting a window into their lives is not healthy.

Dating sites tend to let you know when a user last logged in, whether they're very active, and possibly even show whether they're online. Of course it's not just about investigating how active they are; it's combing their profiles to see what changes they've made, whether it's to photos or to their description, or even setting up a fake profile to see if information can be gleaned. Even discovering that their profile has been removed from the site can be enough to send some people into a tailspin because they panic and believe that the removal means that they've moved on to another relationship.

I find that alumni sites tend to be checked when you're both in the same alumni and may be concerned that they're moving on to someone else from your class or that they're sharing information about you, although with the dominance of Facebook, alumni sites are less of a concern.

Forums are full of people gathered around a particular subject and some people do resort to signing up so that they can monitor their ex, even if they're not saying anything about the relationship. When an ex comments via their own name on sites or you're aware of their pseudonym, it can also be tempting to frequent sites that they read and ensure that they haven't got a flirtation going on with another commenter. Or to engage with them anonymously. Which is weird and out of bounds because remember, you're NC and you want some boundaries!

These are of course just *some* examples and really it comes down to avoiding doing things online that connect you to your ex or basically involve you virtually stalking them… and that includes running credit checks (yes really) or even poking around on their work site. Don't feed the curiosity monster because you can lose hours, if not *days* of your life combing the internet for information about your ex and all you're doing is torturing yourself and engaging in what could potentially become compulsive behaviour if you don't get yourself in check.

Snogs, Shags, Cuddles etc

Surprise, surprise, but once you embark on NC, it's time for the bodily contact to stop. Really. I'm not talking about bumping into them or having to see them at work or whatever; I'm talking about bumping bodily parts. You might think, "Well *obviously!*", but you'd be amazed how many people have said stuff to me along the lines of, "Well we only went to first base so it was 'low contact'..." (it's worrying when people old enough to remember when Michael Jackson was black use the term "first base"), "We didn't have full sex and normally we would so it's not fully breaking NC" (Is this like being a little bit pregnant?) and "I am NC but I get lonely sometimes and so I meet up with him for cuddles" (because that screams boundaries, right?).

If sex can be used as a weapon *in* relationships, it can certainly be used *outside* of one too.

They may be the best sex you've ever had, or you may be feeling lonely, but it doesn't mean that you should keep going back for extra helpings. Nobody ever died from lack of sex and really, your vagina or penis definitely shouldn't be the boss of you, as aside from the fact that it's a sexual organ, it's also not a good judge of character. It just doesn't *have* those skills.

NC means no sex, no quick fumbles, slippery snogs, one last shag for old time's sake, or any bodily contact.

I've advised many readers over the years to avoid getting involved with someone who is fresh out of a breakup, certainly for at least the first month but depending on how long it's taking to 'finalise' the breakup, it could be a few months. Why? Because as you may already know, when you first break up with somebody, the conversations and possibly arguments continue, there's calling (or texting/emailing) one another to 'check in' and there's highly likely to be some sort of sexual contact during this period.

I suggest you get the "one last shag for old time's sake" out of the way (if that's on the cards) and then focus on NC. If you've had a lot of these shags (or kisses or cuddles), I would just get on with NC because there is no tipping point of kissing, cuddling and sexing that's suddenly going to make you confident about biting the NC bullet. What are you hoping for? That it's mediocre? I wouldn't rely on this anyway as you'd be surprised how many people keep breaking NC to go back for what essentially boils down to crap sex…

I appreciate why sex etc, may be attractive because it's a 'connection' with someone who is familiar but if a sexual connection was enough to keep a relationship together, you wouldn't be reading this book. The likelihood is that when you 'soothe' yourself with kissing, cuddling or sex with your ex, it's in response to not being able to deal with uncomfortable feelings or not having more appropriate means of dealing with stress, rejection, boredom, horniness or even hunger.

It's also important to note that prioritising sex and allowing yourself to be used for it or even going back for it because it's what they're good at, is *objectification*.

Reconnecting in this manner can string out an unhealthy relationship for months or even years and it's prolonging the agony. When all is said and done and you wake up and realise that you haven't really progressed emotionally, mentally or physically, you'll realise that it wasn't worth exchanging your life and wellbeing for kisses, cuddles and sex, especially when you didn't have a healthy relationship or your self-esteem in tow.

Occasions

Birthdays, Easter, Valentines, Thanksgiving, Christmas/The Holidays, National Curry Day, the FA Cup Final, the birth of a baby, bereavements, anniversaries and the list goes on; there are clearly a *lot* of reasons we can find to get in touch with an ex.

These occasions can catch us off guard because they mark a passage of time that may highlight and even accentuate the differences between the present and where you were at that time the previous year. Sometimes it's not that you're remembering, more that you're experiencing the grief that comes with the hopes you had for being with them for this occasion (it might have been the first) not being realised.

The disappointment is understandable but part of grieving the loss of a relationship and respecting boundaries – both theirs and your own – is recognising that you can't pick up the relationship or restart contact for occasions. You've got to know where to draw the line.

Birthdays and various other occasions in the calendar don't change. Start as you mean to go on because where does it all end with saluting them on each occasion? What are you going to do in year 2 or year 10?

No Contact means… No Contact and if you choose to make contact for any of these reasons, there must be no underlying motive, which there rarely isn't. Feeling compelled to reach out on big occasions is code for *looking for reasons to be in contact* aka *smoke signals*. Some of these 'occasions' are symbols of aspects of your ex that form part of your connection which in turn you attach a meaning to. So, for example, when their team wins in a big sporting event, that can set off the temptation to reach out.

These occasions become opportunities to ensure that you haven't been forgotten and to place yourself front and centre in their mind. Really, is a card or a message going to make this person change or regret missing you, race back into your life and sweep you off your feet?

Occasions can also represent waiting for an excuse or a bad situation to befall them that you can exploit. Hard to hear but if you could see my inbox! Really, you shouldn't be waiting for the perfect excuse to try and get your agenda on the table. I get it and understand that you're grieving and that you miss them, but this all goes back to validating the original reasons for doing NC and getting behind your decision. It's a totally normal part of the breakup to be reminded of your ex by certain things –

this dissipates over time as long as you don't use these memories to inflate meaning or your hurt.

Take a bereavement for instance – I totally understand why you might want to reach out at this time but there a couple of things that reveal where you're really at: your *method* of expressing your condolences and what you *expect* or *do* after these condolences have been expressed. Best way to express your condolences? Send a card and flowers, pick up the phone, or go around and pay your respects if there is an open house or a set time to do so. Sending a text or posting something on their Facebook page? Come on now!

Equally, if all you're doing is a genuine expression of your condolences, there shouldn't be any thinking about getting back together, sleeping with them, or feeling that you have to stick around to get them through this time because you're not in their life anymore and you're not the only person capable of providing support, especially because you're supposed to be NC. If they try it on with you, don't tell them all about themselves but do just say, "I'm sorry for your loss and that you're hurting. I wanted to let you know this but it doesn't mean that I want to restart anything with you. Take care"… and… move it along. With this in mind, here are some more tips for navigating these situations:

1. Don't hijack the occasion. I've heard enough painful stories of exes that suddenly got back in touch around a bereavement, birthday etc, swooped in with a whole load of big promises and showboating, acted like they were The Most Supportive Partner Ever™… and then vanished off the face of the earth. There are too many people who associate the painful loss of their parent or a milestone birthday with an ex. You're supposed to be NC so you shouldn't be hijacking anyway.

2. When it's *their* birthday, it's not *your* birthday. If you're mostly thinking about your own internal drama, you're not really thinking about *him/her* and you are in fact *projecting*. It being their birthday is not a valid reason for breaking NC because it's like trying to give *yourself* some sort of birthday present in the form of validation and possibly attempting to rekindle the relationship. Birthdays only last for one day but the effects of misplaced expectations and unhealthy habits last far longer.

3. Avoid starting NC within a few days to a couple of weeks of their (or your) birthday because the likelihood is, you'll reach out. In fact, this really applies to most occasions but birthdays in particular because they're personal. If it's your birthday and you start NC and they don't get in touch and it's only been a short time since starting NC, you may feel compelled to tell them all about themselves or go attention seeking. If it's their birthday, you may feel "bad" about not being in touch. Have an honest conversation with yourself – if you think that you're highly likely to knee-jerk into contact if you start NC and then a birthday happens later in the week, wait until *afterwards* and spare yourself (and them) the drama.

4. Be careful of feeling compelled to reach out on anniversaries. I understand it, believe me, especially if you were together through something difficult like a bereavement, but working through this anniversary without them and possibly with the support of others, is grief work that you need to focus on. Yes they may understand you and you them and yes, you may feel bonded over this difficult situation, but it's not enough to cancel out the reasons why you're doing NC. You have to find a way to start dealing with this.

5. You don't *need* to send a card. Whether it's for a birthday, Christmas or whatever, the fact that you're even thinking about sending a card demonstrates that you are still too concerned with how you look and so-called 'protocol' instead of putting your energies into NC.

6. Remember that sending messages to their friends and family on big occasions may be perceived as you sending a smoke signal to your ex. I appreciate that you may like their family for instance, but be careful of not only crossing your ex's boundaries, but also of inadvertently maintaining a connection between you both.

7. Your message, whatever guise it takes, may be disruptive. It's bad enough when they mess with your head, but actually, being NC and then reaching out sends *mixed messages*. There is also the not-so-small matter of the possibility that they may be involved with someone else and that you sending messages as if you have some sort of claim on them even though ironically, you're NC, may create friction and cross boundaries.

8. Don't send a gift. 'Nuff said.

9. If you're thinking about sending a text, email or tippy tapping out a Facebook message, you're just not *that* serious about sending a message. Yes I'm sure these feel 'easier' but again, if you're that worried about avoiding conflict and not opening yourself up to hurt, stick to NC.

10. Think ahead. NC is very much about getting conscious, thinking ahead and planning for success instead of planning for failure. Each year has occasions in the calendar – how are you going to deal with these? They're inevitable so there's no point in being surprised by them. Put a message in your diary or calendar to remind you to stick to NC and if you know that you get card angst, put reminders in your phone in the days running up to the date to keep you on the right track, like "Remember! It's not *my* birthday" or "Make plans on _____ so that I don't feel lonely and vulnerable".

Mutual Friends and Friends of Your Ex's

Genuine mutual friends are people with whom you *both* share friendships *mutually*, which is different to friends of theirs that you've become acquainted with but they're essentially still *their* friends. It doesn't matter how well you feel that you get on with them because if you don't have a friendship that exists or can move to exist beyond your involvement with your ex, you maintaining contact with these people will only open you up to pain that you can afford to miss out on.

Whether it's that they're genuine mutual friends or acquaintances you've met via your ex, how you handle these people has the potential to affect not only your emotional health during this time, including anxiety levels, but also how successful you are at making NC stick.

Fears around 'protocol' and conflict may have you scared of addressing this situation and pre-empting the potential for a conflict of interest with your ex, but addressing this issue sooner rather than later will serve NC best. There's also an added benefit – it's very easy for so-called mutual friends and acquaintances to form a skewed opinion of you when you appear to be bang smack in the middle of drama with your ex and sharing all sorts of stories, so by distancing yourself and/or effectively taking the high road, you end up gaining far more respect, especially if your ex is running their mouth.

1. Don't hang out with these people just to babysit your reputation. Aside from the fact that people are going to think and do what they want to *regardless* of whether you're living in their pockets, it's not very good for your psyche to spend your time on edge and people pleasing. That, and you have way better things to do with your time.

2. Remove the shit stirrers. If a person has contributed to drama between you and your ex, distance yourself immediately, which includes removing them from Facebook if you're connected there. If after the breakup they've proven to be disruptive, quietly distance yourself if possible.

3. Minimise the potential to hear gossip. Instruct all mutual friends not to come to you with any information about your ex, unless they have 'the clap' or some other such STD that affects your health. You need to move on, not hear out-of-context information where people make more out of something than actually exists.

4. Avoid fishing for information. Believe me, it never sounds as casual as you think it does and you may give the impression that your conversation has all been a preamble to the main agenda – getting information about your ex. The first few times you don't ask, it can feel excruciating but it gets easier. This also has the added benefit of ensuring that should you end up being wounded by something you hear about your ex, at least you'll know that it wasn't due to your own rampant curiosity.

5. Don't hold yourself hostage to uncomfortable conversations. If your friends are your friends, they'll have a modicum of decency and realise that it's of no benefit for you to hear about how your ex is shagging around, their relationship isn't working out, or that they look sad. Will you thank them when you not only fall off the wagon but discover that nothing much has really changed? Rather than continue to feel wounded each time your ex is brought up in conversation, bite the bullet and say, "I know you mean well but I really would rather not hear about _____ (whatever it is that they've just said)" or change the subject as soon as possible without contributing an opinion.

6. If the 'friendship' enables you to maintain a flimsy connection to your ex, it's a form of keeping contact! You may have genuine intentions at this time but don't be afraid to have an honest conversation with yourself and evaluate the authenticity of your friendship further down the line. If it becomes clear that a lot of what binds you *is* your ex and talking about them, for the sake of your emotional peace, refocus your energy on your own friendships. I know all of this because I've done it and not only is it not fair on the person who thinks that you want to be friends (you're using them no matter which way you look at it) but you're also deluding yourself and stalling the process of moving on.

7. Don't expect or even demand that they side with you – this is validation seeking. Yes, your ex may well be a jackass but that doesn't mean that you have the right to hijack their friendships or to attempt to force their friends to see them in a negative light. This is crossing boundaries and the harder you try to convince them, the more you look like you're protesting too much and it starts to look like *you're* the problem. Just because they're friends, it doesn't mean that they agree with your ex's behaviour but even if they do, all that does is show that you have incompatible values and that you can't be friends.

8. Avoid meeting up with genuine mutual friends until you're in a stronger position. Sometimes hanging out triggers nostalgia or at the very least, what can result in a very painful outpouring of grief, which in turn may have you reaching out to your ex if you're particularly vulnerable. Hanging out and having a good time can give you a false sense of security that maybe things weren't 'that bad' and that you've been 'too harsh', 'too hasty' or too something. That said, if they really are true friends, bite the bullet and hang out – it gets easier and easier each time and they will understand.

9. Don't get embroiled in drama when you're out socially. Whether it's dirty looks, staring and then laughing or whispering, awkward accusations or full-on confrontations, it all ends up looking a bit like you're auditioning for Jerry Springer. You can politely say hello, have a brief conversation and move away to someone else, smile and wave and then refocus on speaking to whoever you're with, or leave if you think it's going to blow up.

Family

If you've gotten to know your ex's family and have actually become quite fond of, and close to, them, the truth is that you have to break up with them too. It doesn't mean that you're never going to be in touch again but what you and they have to recognise is that you can't all continue on as if the breakup never happened or that your ex's feelings don't matter.

Maintaining a relationship with them and even discussing your ex could end up tapping into feelings of rejection and abandonment for your ex and the truth is, there is a *boundary* issue. They may feel like your family too (and they may be if you both share children) but it's important to remember that NC is about inserting some boundaries into your life, breaking habits and establishing new patterns so that you can move forward.

1. If you're close with their family, do call /visit them/send an email (but not a text) and let them know that you're going to be out of touch for a while. Tell them that you've loved getting to know them and the times that you've shared etc, but that you need to take some time out to come to terms with the loss of the relationship. *Don't* be derogatory about your ex even if they appear to side with you.

2. They may ask for reasons but you don't *have* to go into detail about why you're doing NC. Instead of providing very specific, detailed reasons you can say something like, "The breakup has been really hard for both of us and for me, I'm realising that being in touch/trying to make it work again is causing me too much pain. Who knows? We [you and your ex] may be able to be friends later down the line but it's not possible at the moment."

3. If you're going to explain, keep it to three points and *short*. Remember that if you get into nitty gritty details, you may end up not only feeling like you have to argue these points but you may be revealing sensitive information. For instance, they may be unaware that your ex has been abusing drugs and alcohol. That said, if your ex has been engaging in dangerous behaviour (abusive, stalking, addiction etc), them knowing may keep your ex at bay. *That* said, it may anger your ex and aggravate further behaviour.

4. Don't get sucked in by being guilted or their rationalisations or even protestations that your ex needs you to be a better person or whatever. They weren't in your relationship, it's not up to them to determine what you can or 'should' handle, and it's not up to you to save your ex, which would make it an incredibly unhealthy, codependent relationship. They are your ex's family – they need to take responsibility for providing support instead of micromanaging your input to avoid stepping up.

5. Don't stress if they do get in touch. Remember they may feel a bit attached to you (hey you're a likeable person!) and they will have to go through their own grieving process which is helped by the boundaries that you're building during the NC process. But do request that they don't pass information about your ex to you or vice versa.

Of course it may be that it's a member of your family that's been in touch with your ex and this can also represent boundary issues especially if it appears like the family member is discounting your version of events or seems to have little regard for your feelings. It may feel like they're taking sides as there may be an expectation that now that you're broken up, their connection 'should' end too.

This situation is tricky and it depends on a number of factors including your relationship with the family member, whether they're regarding it as something that they don't want to get involved in, whether they are clear on the issues, and what type of relationship they have with your ex. If they were friends or professionally involved prior to your involvement, it can be tricky to say 'pick sides' even if technically they 'should' because you're family. It can be even trickier if they're either not fully aware of what happened between you and so think that you're being 'dramatic' or something, or they *are* fully aware but possibly being sympathetic and even supportive with your ex.

There is no easy way to handle this situation and it's something that you have to feel your way around. While treating this situation like the 'mutual friends' situation may help to a degree, this is likely to only go so far if your relationship with the family member(s) is strained or even fraught.

If your relationship with your ex is what I would regard as a 'code red' relationship, i.e. there is verbal, emotional or physical abuse, addiction, boundary-busting behaviour or basically anything that amounts to being treated without love, care, trust and respect, you may need to quietly distance yourself from your family.

You should be able to explain your reasons in a brief or even detailed manner (they are your family after all) but the truth is, if the dynamic in your family is unhealthy and may actually play a part in why you might be involved with your ex in the *first* place, they won't 'get' the fact that you don't want to continue your involvement. They may feel that being in a volatile relationship is normal so you making a different, *healthier* choice may cause them to feel uncomfortable, which incidentally, isn't your problem. Your ex may also have charmed your family (abusive types can be very manipulative and divisive) which is all the more reason to keep a record of everything they say and do.

1. Explain your reasons but don't look for their *permission*. You don't need their permission to end your own relationship or to hold the perspective that you do.

2. Try to stick to brief explanations. If you're inclined to be a people pleaser with your family, I would keep your explanation brief (the 3-pointer) and ensure that you're completely clear on your *own* reasons for doing NC so it doesn't feel like you're trying to convince them *and* you. This also ensures that you cannot be talked around. "I appreciate your point of view but I've already done a lot of thinking on this and I've given this as much of a try as possible and it's time for me to step back. I hope that you can try to understand my decision and I would really appreciate your support, but also appreciate that you're friends with them and I'm not seeking to interfere with this".

3. Do request that they don't chat about your private business to your ex. If you already know that there's a 'leak', I would do yourself a favour and not let them know anything that you wouldn't want them passing to your ex. You can take the route of stressing yourself out over their chatterbox ways and saying "I should be able to tell my own family _____" or you can respect who this person is or isn't and adjust accordingly instead of setting yourself up for pain. People 'should' do a lot of things… but they don't. If you know that they've got a big mouth, I wouldn't even bother asking them not to say anything because their indignation at you even asking coupled with your vulnerability may trigger their big mouth. If they don't have anything, they'll be free to make it up or poke around.

4. Try to find out if they're being invited to something but don't raise hell over it. Assuming that you've already let them know that you're no longer in touch with your ex, don't waste your time explaining. If you let them know ahead of time that you're changing your mind about going, there will be this big drama about trying to get you to change your mind. Next thing you have people pulling the 'maturity' card. If they show up, keep a polite distance and if it's too much, quietly make an exit. At the end of the day, what does this family member expect? A red carpet welcome?

5. Don't allow your family to pass messages. This is when things can become very juvenile so the best thing is to nip it in the bud and remind them that you don't want to hear about or from them, or just don't respond.

6. You may need to be frank with your kids, especially if they're teenagers. Sometimes your child knows a relationship partner and may even have a level of affection for them or even feel particularly bonded if their other parent isn't around. You don't need to go into immense detail with your child but after hearing from quite a few parents whose children have been manipulated by ex-partners who have tricked them into letting them into their home or giving out their parents new number, it would be remiss of me not to emphasise the importance of protecting your safety. It's sad that another person would attempt to compromise your child but if you do find that your ex is attempting to get to you via your child or has already tried to, it's time to slam down the boundary gauntlet.

❖ There's no need to scare the bejaysus out of them but do stress to your child that there are some issues that mean that it's important that they don't pass your information to your ex or to let them into your home.

❖ If you let your ex know that you're going NC, do ask that they respect it and not attempt to approach you through your kids.

❖ Agree a password that you will give to someone who you've made an arrangement with to come to your home. If your ex claims that they're meeting you at your home, your child can ask for the password and it won't seem so strange if this is something that's put into practice across the board.

❖ If your ex is approaching your children (and they're not adults), consider this to be serious and note any and all approaches and speak with your local law enforcement about your options.

Dealing With Possessions

NC or no NC, breakups often involve the not so small matter of dealing with possessions, both returning theirs and getting yours back. For the sake of your own emotional health and the tendency to get nostalgic when it's a tough day, it's better to deal with the possessions issue from the outset rather than leave it. If there's going to be wrangling, better to get it out of the way *now* and know exactly where you stand – do not save up the discussion about possessions as a future potential opening for making contact because actually, it's what shady types tend to do in order to leverage it and gain control.

If you are serious about cutting contact and don't want to engage in any game playing, sort out possessions pronto. Don't start NC in haste and then have to organise possessions at leisure, not least because it's bloody stressful and will undermine your efforts.

One of the things that giving or taking back possessions does if you haven't started NC, is act as final communication that can help those of you with a tendency to want to say what is on your mind. If you've been thinking, "I should tell them I'm going NC", asking for your possessions or leaving them at their place will take care of this discussion.

I must reiterate: don't use giving back or taking possessions as a way to open up a dialogue because it is unlikely to yield anything other than conflict that will still end up causing you to do NC, only now you have even more headache than you started out with. In fact, it may even stall the process if you spend enough time listening because you may get nostalgic or believe excuses and decide to do One Last Chance Again. That aside, you still need to deal with possessions.

For a start, go through every room in your home and cleanse your place of *everything* that either 1) belongs to this person or 2) are mementos of your relationship.

Be rigorous in the cleanse and for the time being focus on picking up everything. You can sort it out once you've gathered them all and put them together. If you're feeling very upset, it may help to have a friend with you but choose a friend that will be kind but 'no nonsense' and get on with the job at hand. You don't need someone confusing the issue or trying to distract you from your intentions. I know you're probably feeling crappy, but put on some music and treat it like a cleaning session. The sooner it's over, the sooner you can reclaim your space.

WHAT TO RETURN

- Anything of value whether that's monetary value, or they're crazy about it, or it technically belongs to someone else, for example it was loaned to them or it belongs to a friend or family member, or is even an heirloom.

- Give back CDs, books, iPods, iPads, laptops, TVs, cameras, mobile phones, their photos and other mementos/possessions. If they have toiletries that are of value (i.e. they're proper cosmetics with a proper name on them and they're at least half full), include these as well.

- Return clothing (no need to wash and iron) and that includes any you purchased. I wouldn't kill yourself looking for the missing feet of odd socks, and even though you could easily throw out dirty underwear, for a personal giggle, you can always package it up with their stuff.

- Engagement rings should be returned unless they've already told you to keep it. If it's the latter option, I'd look into your selling options... They make for a nice little holiday. I intended to sell my old one, forgot about it, and then sold it a few weeks before my wedding several years later and the cash came in very handy – thank you very much ex!

RETURNING THEIR STUFF

- Either call, send an email, or let them know when you're face-to-face (assuming that you're currently still around one another) and provide two dates and times for collection (or drop off) of their possessions. If you leave it vague, *they'll* possibly be vague too. Offering a couple of dates and times means that they either have to pick one or suggest an alternative.

- If for whatever reason they don't collect the items, send one reminder email requesting that they collect the items by a certain date (this ensures that you've got proof should an issue arise further down the line) and that if they don't, you will assume that they no longer need the items and they'll be passed to charity. Note, if you've started NC, it doesn't mean you've broken it by having to send the reminder. An alternative is to return the items to their friend, especially if they're dodging collecting them or providing you with somewhere to send it.

- Peace of mind is priceless so if you can afford it and it's a matter of a small amount of items, box up the stuff and send it by post/courier – make sure it's signed for so that they can't claim it wasn't received or get proof of postage. Or drop them off when they're not around (put in a sheltered area like a porch or bag up in a labelled refuse sack). If it's small, you can send it to their office. Note that a lot of courier companies take a mobile/cell number and get in touch with the recipient a few hours beforehand which means that there really is no reason why your ex cannot take receipt of their own property.

- If they start down the whole claiming that they've left something at yours, make sure that they give you a list of everything at that point so that they don't keep pulling the same moves. I've heard from a woman whose ex calls up every couple of months or so, or harangues her with texts about missing spoons! They've been broken up well over a year!

- Getting a list of stuff from them at the outset will also make it easier for you to pack up.

- If you pack up their stuff without their assistance, inventory it and take photos of any valuable items so that you cannot be blamed for any damage.

- If there's a lot of stuff, agree a date and time for them to come around and take everything, and then make yourself scarce while you're there. I know some people who get their parent or a friend to keep an eye on things and it spares you from having awkward conversations.

- Don't purposefully damage or even destroy items because aside from being vengeful, it's also illegal.

RETRIEVING YOUR STUFF

- If you haven't broken up yet or you haven't moved out, I would start organising your stuff and removing any sentimental or valuable items if possible, especially if you have genuine concerns that they may do something to them (like destroy or sell them) behind your back. You could ask a trusted friend or family member to take care of the items or you could also put them into short-term storage. If you haven't broken up yet though, do be careful of removing so much stuff that you alert them before you've let them know.

- Suggest a couple of days and times when you can go to their place or they can drop off. Do it by email or phone and of course you can follow it up with texts. State in the communication that if they cannot do either of those days and times, to suggest a couple of alternatives.

- If you don't want to see them (this is understandable), arrange for a courier or a good friend to collect the items on a specific day and time.

- It's your responsibility to ensure that if you're not collecting the stuff, that you provide as comprehensive a list as possible for the person who is collecting/packing it up.

- Don't do it in dribs and drabs aka stalling the retrieval to maintain contact.

- Do make sure you hold onto any important receipts, just in case they make a claim for an item that you know is yours.

- If they won't return something and it's of sentimental value or it's straight up valuable, you may have to go down the legal route especially if you have records of this person saying that they would return it as well as the receipts or any other proof of ownership. It's tough because I've heard from people whose exes wouldn't return items that were given or made for them by loved ones who have passed away but there comes a point when you will have to weigh up the financial and emotional cost of pursuing this person for it. They can't take your memories and sometimes, when they finally twig that they have no hold over you and that you're willing to let it go, they return it.

- Don't vandalise their property while packing up. Yes this should go without saying but I actually know of two people who peed all over an ex partners stuff and cut up all of their clothes. And yes they did end up in court.

JOINT POSSESSIONS

- Have this discussion (some people do it via email if face-to-face or on the phone is proving too acrimonious) prior to NC. This is something natural that happens as part of a breakup or separation.
- Everything will need to be inventoried, something you may have already done as part of the breakup.
- Items that you've purchased together will need to be divided up appropriately which may be based on value or attachment.
- If there's a legal process involved such as sale of a property or a divorce, you may find it easier to do it through your solicitors or a mediator, although obviously it costs less if you can sort it out amicably between yourselves. I probably wouldn't mention that you intend to do NC prior to this discussion as it's just going to aggravate the situation.

WHAT TO BOX AWAY FOR A RAINY DAY –
MEMORY TRIGGERS & SOME GIFTS

- Get a shoe box and put away all the 'nostalgia gear' you've amassed – concert and cinema tickets, photos, that chipped tea mug, and basically anything that evokes memories of them.

- Take down photos, remove passport photo out of your purse or wallet etc.

- There are other things that you may have been given by them such as clothing, jewellery, books, electrical goods, whatever – these are yours although you may not be ready to use any of them.

- Now… if you're going to lose your mind every time you put on that top, or that bracelet, or go past that book, get a bigger box and put them all away until you're in a better place. You may find when you take them out that you want to sell them on eBay (or similar) or donate to your local charity shop.

- If you feel emotionally attached it should go in the box, if you don't, it should go in the bin. Or you can repurpose it – you know upcycling is all the rage. Get that sofa recovered, customise that shirt – get creative, they're yours!

ABOUT THAT HOMEMADE PORNO OR THE SEXY
SNAPS

Bet you thought I'd missed this!

- Let me assure you that there's no need to watch yourself having sex with your ex, but I do suggest that you box up your homemade videos and saucy photos and put them in a safe place that only you know about, preferably locked. Or burn, shred or bust them up.

- Of course we're in a digital age so you might not have a (cough) hard copy of your images or videos. Delete, delete and delete. If you do decide to keep it on your computer (I would caution you against keeping it on your phone especially if you're prone to losing it), make sure that your computer is password protected and it's filed away safely. I'll put it this way – I wouldn't label the file as "[your name] porno".

- If you have a discussion about dividing up possessions, you can ask for their copy of the tape/pics but some things are better left unsaid as you put ideas in their head and open up a dialogue, plus you potentially offer them a way of having power over you.

- If you bring it up, do it in a calm, casual but firm manner and do not betray even a drop of desperation because it's like offering up the blueprints to screw you over.

- If you previously discussed what would happen to videos or photos if you broke up, refer to the discussion and try to be as specific as possible.

- If you're still living together at this point or in the process of organising moving out, you could (politely) make the request and supervise the removal. Don't bother falling for this "Don't you trust me to remove it?" It's not about trust; it's about ending the relationship properly and not feeling reliant on an external party having the sole responsibility to do something and you not being in a position to supervise or check up on it. It's the type of thing that should be done immediately or ASAP, not any of this "I'll get to it soon" BS.

- If all else fails and you have genuine concerns that your ex is going to distribute the material or is already blackmailing you, seek legal advice immediately – a letter may scare them off.

POST

- Get your post redirected. I don't know how many people I come across complaining about how they end up speaking because their ex has forgotten to sort out their mail. Stop! It is your responsibility to sort this and many use it as an excuse for contact. It's relatively cheap to pay your postal service to redirect your mail automatically. Otherwise, give extremely specific instructions to your ex and make sure they're agreed, not assumed. Make life easy and provide self-addressed, stamped envelopes but really, get the redirection and your address change sorted.

- Request that they arrange a redirect and/or change their address. If you have to post stuff, don't do it in dribs and drabs – agree a set period of once a week for a month or so which gives them time to notify companies/arrange a redirect. If they're expecting you to post their stuff, they should volunteer the postage but don't hold your breath if they don't.

- If, let's say, three months have gone by and it's still turning up, stop posting it. You can also do Return To Sender.

- Don't accept packages from delivery people.

Get a Sponsor/Buddy

This can be that one person that you can rely on to sanity check things, who you can call up or meet up with when you feel weak. This works particularly well if you've previously being suffering alone and in secret. Explain that you're cutting contact and that you really need some extra support right now, and get them on board with giving a shoulder to lean on. Don't worry about being a pain – most people have experienced heartbreak and one day, you'll have the opportunity to pay it forward with someone else. Your true friends would rather hear from you than have you suffer. There does need to be some boundaries for both of you and I suggest you choose someone with some compassion and objectivity, not an enabler who is going to encourage you to break NC because they don't recognise unhealthy relationships. You need to be able to call on this person in your dark moments and be able to be honest without fear of judgement.

If you've been keeping what has been happening a secret, it's time to ask someone for help and tell them what's been going on. Don't tell someone who has a tendency to be judgemental. Choose someone who will be honest, but with love behind it. You don't have to tell them every nitty itty gritty detail but you should tell them enough for them to realise that you need some hand-holding.

Make sure they have a little free time each day (or however often you feel is needed) to catch up, and make sure they're OK with being called up even if it's late at night. Make sure they are OK with you talking about him/her and the relationship, especially if this is someone who you have already bent the ear off telling them chapter and verse of everything that is happening in your life.

You may feel that you've overstayed your welcome with certain friends because of everything that has been said previously, or because they have repeatedly told you what a tool the guy is, but you may need to step back and be objective and be humble enough to say "OK, they were the things you said, but I needed to find out the hard way, and I could really appreciate your support right now". Being friends is not about always being right or feeling that the other person must and should take advice. We have to make our own mistakes because we'll second-guess ourselves if the choice is not ours. It may have been very obvious to all of those around you that you needed to get out of the relationship, but because you were emotionally invested and were not ready to 'hear' and 'see', you needed more time.

A word of caution though: if you have exhausted your credit with a friend, while it is hurtful, don't flip out about it and do empathise with their position. They may be afraid of stepping into this due to how things have previously played out. It's very tough to be the friend in a situation where your friend is in a destructive relationship, complains about it and then doesn't do anything or keeps going back so it may take a bit of time for your friend to realise that you're serious. It's not fair to be mad at them for wanting to take their time because the truth is, you need to give it time to show that this isn't the same as last time and it's best to do this with actions, not words.

If you have a friend who has experienced their own pain and come out the other side, speak to them. So many people have experienced their own heartache; don't make snap judgements and assume that they won't understand or that no one has been through what you've been through. You'd be surprised!

If your options are limited friendship-wise and your friends are in their own drama, do make clear to them that going back is not an option and that if they can't accept that, they should say so from the outset so that you know where you stand. You don't need someone undermining your decision!

Don't abuse the support by turning into a broken record and expecting them to sit there for months on end whilst you refuse to grieve and move forward. While you don't need them badgering you about getting over your ex, there's really a limit to how much you should expect someone to hold your hand for, especially if you don't want to end up in a different kind of codependent relationship.

I encourage you to get plenty of support in the first month to three months but you will recognise if you are progressing or stalling the hands of change and grief, or if you find you don't need them so much, don't want to talk about him so much, or on the flip side, find yourself being increasingly dependent on them.

Don't be selfish either and do try to take an interest in their lives. It'll do you good to talk about something other than 'him/her' or 'us'. Don't censor yourself but do look for other things to talk about. Many readers have shared that they realised that they were on the way to healing and wanting to progress when they didn't want to talk about it all the time or to surround themselves with people who wanted to keep rehashing the past.

LOW CONTACT & TRICKY SITUATIONS

There are some instances when 'can't' is more like 'won't' break up or go NC – like when you break up and then find yourself lured back in like a moth to a flame. However, there *are* some circumstances and people where you have to have some level of contact with them. Much as you might not want to, for the foreseeable future or even for the long-term due to sharing children, you're going to have to deal with them.

While full NC is a necessity for certain types of relationships and people, and also for self-protection when you're engaging in damaging behaviour, there are actually variations of No Contact that you have done before without realising it. The most common example is when you've experienced a breakup, kept in touch for the first few weeks or so and then it's petered out as you've both got on with your respective lives. One or both of you realise that space is needed to come to terms with things and it's just left alone. It's also the same when you stop making an effort with a particular friend or you're busy each time a colleague who has crossed the line a few times with you, asks you out to lunch.

Low Contact is the form of NC that's needed when you're going to have to continue seeing this person due to circumstance, such as working together, sharing a child or the finalising of money and legal concerns. You'll always know that it's *legitimate* Low Contact if you're engaging *only* to the degree that's needed in order to facilitate whatever it is that's needed to be done. If it's not specifically and directly related to your child/work/documentation and is instead about engaging to get the relationship back or to seek validation etc, that's not low contact *or* NC. Basically Low Contact is doing NC but instead of cutting off entirely, it's not engaging beyond the very specific reason that you can't do full NC.

This means that if you're contemplating cutting contact with your ex-husband/wife, the person you're separated from, family, friends who you may still need to see around, co-workers, the father/mother of your child, you can cut contact with them, not by cutting them entirely out of your life, but by consistently communicating your new boundaries so that they realise that if they want to engage with you, they need to do so in a manner which respects your boundaries or you won't be engaging. People recognise consequences through actions, particularly if the person or people in question are used to you talking but not following through. Taking decisive action is far more effective.

This section also covers tricky situations including money issues, recovery from a fantasy involvement and dealing with someone who is abusive or even a narcissist with a chapter on The Get Out Plan for if you need to have a carefully managed exit for your own protection.

CO-PARENTING

Having children adds a new dimension to No Contact but the principles remain the same – you're not cutting contact between your ex and your child; you're cutting it between the two of you and keeping it politely distant. Let me reassurance you that this isn't impossible, you just need to factor in your ex remaining a part of your life, but that it's got to be all about your child from now on.

Whenever I see people who have kids struggling with NC, it's because they either don't believe that they have NC as an option or it's because they confuse the fact that they have to co-parent with their ex with having rights to continue drama. Many parents worry about the effect of breaking up but at the same time many don't give enough thought to the effect of them remaining together. I've come across so many people who are the adult children of parents who repeatedly broke up and got back together, or who had incredibly unhealthy relationships, or even worse, claimed that they remained in toxic relationships *for* the children. No child wants or deserves that burden. If you remain in an unhealthy relationship, at least be honest about why you're doing this and don't put it on the child – it will mess with their head as they get older and they may feel very guilty and confused, especially if they know that your self-esteem and quality of life has been very affected.

Ultimately, you're going to have to do 'low contact' – when you engage with your ex, it needs to be about your child, not your ego or your past relationship.

You can limit contact with the parent of your child and unless they're abusive/neglectful to your child – which is another matter altogether – there's no need to treat the fact that you've both broken up as an opportunity to cut your child off from their parent. It's not fair to your child or your ex to use your child as a weapon against them. While there are shady relationship partners who are also shady parents, there are also parents who cannot hold a relationship together and are a pain in the arse, but they do love their children and actually manage to be good parents. Both of you can be the parent of your child even though your relationship isn't continuing.

Prioritise Welfare Not Ego

When you have an unhealthy relationship or you no longer want to be together even if at one point it was a healthy relationship, it's important for all parties concerned that boundaries, consistency, the welfare of your children and your own welfare are considered. It's critical to balance serving the needs of your child with your own needs, wishes and expectations. If you involve your child in the drama or they become increasingly aware of the negative impact upon you, which may include you not being truly emotionally, physically and spiritually available to them, this is a problem.

Judge the situation and make decisions that are appropriate to the wellbeing of your family. Your child loves both of you and may want you both to remain together but they're not schooled in the nuances of adult relationships, nor are they privy to the ins and outs of why your relationship hasn't worked out (and nor do they need to be). If their other parent has been in their life then they're going to feel a difference initially but if you remove yourself out of the drama and focus on co-parenting, they'll gradually feel more secure. If your child is now an adult or close to being an adult, I certainly wouldn't try to remain in an unhealthy relationship at their instruction and don't let them get involved in 'mediating' and 'conflict resolution' because not only will it end in tears but children who feel that they have to Florence Nightingale their parents end up growing up into adults who get involved in codependent relationships and/or become people pleasers with no sense of their own identities.

Stick To Civil As Your Default Setting

Start as you mean to go on – being civil and handling things maturely. You can do this without being bosom buddies. There may come a time when you can relax a bit more and being friendly gets easier but just remember that until you've established a consistent rhythm for co-parenting *and* you're over them *and* they're not overstepping your boundaries, stick to Low Contact. If being polite is made nigh on impossible by their behaviour, go for the absolute bare minimum. I personally know parents who are doing Low Contact and because there's no drama, the children are happy and the parents have been forced to get on with their respective lives, which may include dealing with issues which ultimately benefit the children and their relationship with their ex. If you can both show a united front with your child even if you have to grit your teeth on other subjects, your child will feel secure.

Set Boundaries Now

NC when you have children is about not engaging in all of the stuff that has contributed to the breakdown of the relationship, and focusing on co-parenting. You will send mixed signals to your child if your boundaries aren't put in place asap and the longer that it goes on for, the harder that it is for your child to adapt. Decide what your boundaries are and recognise where you're vulnerable so that you can strengthen boundaries that your ex might typically exploit. If they keep trying to cross the line, send a weekly email that has bullet points of what your child has done each week.

Pre-empt any dodgy moves on their part and put photocopies of report cards, pictures they've done etc, with them in an envelope or bag ready to hand over when you're doing drop off or collection. In fact, if they keep pushing it, you know that they have no interest in you sharing this information, so stop and let them recognise the difference and ask for it. This is always difficult to digest because we're protective of our children and want to believe that their parent has their utmost interest at heart but some people don't. You do. Hopefully they do too and your children will no doubt reap the benefit when dealing with your ex one-on-one, but via you, if they demonstrate that they can't disentangle from their desire to manipulate and control you, hold firm on your boundaries.

Stay On Topic

Keep the overwhelming majority of the conversations on topic (about your child) until you've firmly established the boundaries and they've received the message loud and clear that you are not interested in anything beyond this. The litmus test of this is: you know that you can relax a bit when you've reached indifference and aren't personalising your ex's behaviour and giving away your power.

If your ex uses talk about the kids as an opening to line you up for boundary busting, keep it brief and if they cross the line, feign another call coming through or a place you have to go. Do it every single time and eventually they learn that if they change the topic, you'll end the conversation.

If things are pretty raw, keep the small talk to a minimum. Because your actions are all about NC and co-parenting, this will not cause mixed signals especially because they'll work out through these actions that yes you're being civil, but no you're not engaging beyond this. You don't need to know how they are; they don't need to know how you are. Of course you can ask but it's in that "How are you?" kinda way, not "How are you so by the way are you sleeping with somebody? Are you missing me?" While this may seem harsh, until you're in an emotional place where you don't run the risk of putting yourself at risk for confusion or hurt (by reading too much into things they may be saying or doing) impose a conversational diet. Otherwise you run the risk of being nostalgic, getting things out of perspective, and potentially reacting to this.

Don't Hang About

Aid the process by working out pick up and drop off arrangements that don't leave much room for hanging about. This means being ready on time because waiting around is either going to create an opportunity for conversation or possibly confrontation. You can also open the door when you see them pulling up outside and bring your child out or go outside to collect. The message will be loud and clear – you're not engaging.

Consider Mediation

Meeting with a neutral, professional third party every few weeks for a few months can be incredibly beneficial for not only creating boundaries between you and working out how to co-parent, but it will focus discussions to these sessions so that not only can you can go about your life in the meantime but you can focus on being and doing things that help NC and your mediation sessions. A mediator will focus on ensuring that you reach an agreement that meets your child's needs while also working out the practical side of your breakup and also nipping any unhelpful side discussions in the bud. This will save you a lot of money on court costs plus an agreement can be drafted that, while not legally binding, should further issues arise, can be taken to your solicitor/lawyer so that they have a clear overview of what was previously agreed.

Some people get incredibly defensive about court so a mediator is often a far more palatable option. I wouldn't go to mediation sessions and say "Oh by the way, when we're done here, I'm going to cut you off" – there's no need because whether or not mediation is successful (and hopefully it is), you will know that you've tried and when you go about your own life and stop engaging, your reasons will be clear. It wouldn't make sense to go through mediation, make an agreement and then confuse the hell out of it by returning to old discussions, conflicts or even sex.

Of course if they refuse to go for mediation but you do end up having to go to court, your attempts are highly likely to be regarded very favourably. If in the past when you've attempted to have discussions and resolve issues, this person has been quite aggressive, I would insist on mediation so that it's clear that their behaviour will no longer be tolerated.

Don't Eat the Guilt Cookie

Some people know how to play to your people pleasing instincts. Even when what you're doing is essentially curtailing unhealthy behaviour for the benefit of your child, they'll play into this idea that you're committing some sort of wrongdoing. If you've typically been the equivalent of a high-absorbency-blame kitchen roll, they will exploit this. If they claim that you keeping your distance is hindering their parenting, do remind them that they can be a parent *without* sleeping with, arguing with or controlling you and that you're not preventing a relationship with their child. They can't have it both ways and keep you in an unhealthy relationship – you're not their property.

Stick To An Arrangement

Before you embark on Low Contact, work out visitation arrangements and stick with it. Yes it will take some getting used to, yes it may be a big change for one of you if you're used to being around your child all the time, but you all need this arrangement so that you can begin the transition. If you don't have a routine, you don't know what to expect out of your week which means your ex could be popping up like a Jack-in-the-box *plus* it will be very disruptive for your child. Some people get very resistant to making arrangements because it seems so 'formal' and then when they don't know whether they're coming or going, they regret being afraid of conflict or making things official. Make the arrangement – it's in *all* of your best interests.

No Unannounced Visits

You each have your respective lives to lead and they also cannot carry on as if nothing has changed. If you don't set boundaries on this now, you'll be kicking yourself, especially when you eventually start dating somebody else or it feels like nothing has really changed. I also doubt that showing up unannounced cuts both ways so why allow them to throw their weight around? Change the locks (if you haven't already) and make it clear that if they want to come by, they need to make arrangements with you.

If your ex turns up, find out what they want and then let them know that next time they'll need to make an arrangement with you or say that they can stay for a few minutes and then they'll have to go. If it's happened before, ask them to leave as soon as it's possible without there being a big scene. Right now, you're not in a position to be playing host and if you start trying to be all social, you will let down your guard, and no doubt let down your boundaries. Also take advantage of their arrival to go and run some errands or ask a friend to meet up or just go and do something for yourself!

It's inappropriate for them to tell your child that they're coming over without speaking to you first as it puts you in a compromising position. If your child is of an age where they may feel that they can make arrangements, steer them towards arranging to go to your ex's place or have clear guidelines about how these arrangements should be made and when. If your ex claims that they 'should' be able to see their kids whenever the mood strikes, remind them that you're no longer together, you have your own life, and if the mood does strike, they *still* need to make a call and see if what they've planned is possible. Leave a little room in your childcare arrangements for flexibility but I would also try to by and large stick to what has been agreed. If you're going to revise the agreement, do it after it's had a few months trial or the source of teething issues has been identified.

No Sex

I know that there's history but don't overestimate the value of it and end up providing a license to continue sleeping together. While you can do it, not only are you likely to find that it plays havoc with your mind and creates an uncomfortable situation between you both, but you also risk creating tension that will affect everyone including your child.

Think about whether there is a possibility that you'll get hit up for sex, or that you'll be tempted to chase for it, and pre-empt by reminding yourself of exactly why it's a bad idea, especially if this has already happened before because you can gauge what is likely to result from it. What are you going to do the next time that you feel horny? Work out your plan B. Also consider whether sleeping with your ex is worth the confusion you *or* your child might experience. There is a reason why you're no longer together – don't provide the fringe benefits of being with you without the responsibility. Remember: if you allow sex to be your hook, you're giving someone the blueprints to literally screw you over. If you've already done a 'backsliding special', they'll probably believe that they have you where they want you after sleeping together – little do they realise that you've wised up. They may have had their ego stroke, their sex and have proved to themselves that they can still 'get you' so they may feel confident enough to leave you alone until their next fix, but next time you'll know *exactly* how to deal with them.

Dial Down the Drama

Don't use NC to play games that may create drama. Unless you want your child to think that drama and upheaval is normal and then replicate this in their own adult relationships, what you do now is critical for providing a healthy example. Tempting as it may be, try not to say derogatory things about your ex, don't pass messages, don't put them between the two of you and keep the amount of batshit crazy stuff that they hear or witness to an absolute minimum. Ultimately it's a question of asking, "Is this *one* issue worth it?" because if it's instant gratification and a longer-term hangover, don't go there.

Children don't want to feel divided like they're being made to pick sides or that they're failing you if they love their parent or enjoy spending time with them. They don't want to feel scared and they're also far too young to be having adult concerns and worrying about taking care of you because you don't know how to keep it together. They need consistency even if that consistency is a co-parenting arrangement where the parents aren't the best of friends or even friends at all, but they get on with the business of taking care of their child.

Halt Abuse In Its Tracks

I hear some truly awful stories of exes who seem to think that they can be abusive to the parent of their child. This is completely unacceptable and there are too many parents who feel hostage to an ex's abuse due to sharing a child. You know the signs by now of when they're heading in the abusive direction. Halt things before it even gets that far and keep at a safe distance. Stop expecting this person to be struck by a lightning bolt of conscience and logical reasoning. Stop trying to get them to see your point of view. Stop trying to please this person. Stop accommodating their assholery. Stop giving them airtime. Each and every time they cross the line, create a perceptible consequence – get off the phone, ask them to leave, halt the discussion and make it clear either verbally or through action that you will not be engaging when they pull this stuff with you. Don't keep threatening legal action or mediation – if you say it, follow through. This person is using you as a target to unload their rage, weakness and even self-loathing. They need to stop.

Halt Revisiting Discussions

They may try to draw you into a discussion about why you're being 'formal' (read: not so accommodating) or try to be flirty with you to start the preamble to attempting to cross your boundaries, or they may even try the whole "I miss you". Seeking validation and understanding and/or feeling rejected, coupled with the fact that you both share a child means that you may be tempted to be receptive to this chitchat. If this isn't the first time you've found yourself at this juncture, you must remind yourself of what has happened before and consider and even ask your ex what has truly changed? This has got to be about more than getting confirmation that you're still emotionally there for him/her – you have yourself and your child to think about, so do you really want to be dealing with someone's mixed messages?

Don't be afraid to warn them that if they start this conversation, they need to be able to follow through as you're not prepared to disrupt your own or your children's lives for what could turn out to be a whim. This in itself may be enough to shut them up, however, I would also caution against getting into this discussion until you are several months out of the woods because you may not have enough perspective yet to have worked out what your own needs are and whether you actually want this person. If you're too quick to enter into this discussion, you may let your ego do the talking and the decision-making.

If you've previously fallen off the wagon say, "There's nothing to discuss if this conversation hasn't got something to do with our kids. What happened that time was a mistake and it won't happen again." If they keep pushing it: "I think it's best that we make a different arrangement for collecting/dropping off because it's clear that you are not prepared to respect my wishes/what we've previously agreed" and then go ahead and make the arrangements and let them know about them. They won't like not being in control but you're teaching them that they cannot dictate the terms of everything and effectively have their cake and eat it too.

CO-WORKING

It's unsurprising when you spend a significant portion of your life at work, that the environment is ripe with the opportunity for romantic relationships. Work seems almost 'easier' to meet people because there's an assumption that's often made about common ground and values. You would be surprised at the number of people who believe that somebody is going to make a great relationship partner because they're intelligent, high up, popular, have been in the same job for a long time, or even just assuming that *because* they're working with one another and a romance has started that it means that they'll be treated better and that it's going somewhere.

Work environments *are* handy for meeting people and if it all works out, great, but if it doesn't... well... unless you can get another job (not always an option in the current economy), you'll have to suck it up and put some boundaries between you both so that you can get some breathing space and move on.

While this situation isn't easy, you can make this as big or as small a deal as you want.

The truth is that while you may attach some importance to events like bumping into this person at the copier, the likelihood is that they won't attach the same importance – these events are unlikely to register on their radar and if they do, it's because they realise that they can generate a desired response from you due to the way you then act around them. How you act around this person can end up communicating that you're *still* into them and for some people, that's more than enough. While initially during NC they may assume that you're not engaging due to being crazy about them, if you stick to your guns, they will gradually realise that you have become indifferent – trust me, I know this from experience!

No Contact is about breaking the contact and habits that facilitate the relationship. Work means that you have to approach things from a practical and professional level so as not to actually hinder your career. You're not breaking NC by sharing a copier or an office – you break NC if you decide the fact that you share a copier and an office is a reason to engage with this person or to even restart the relationship.

Only engage on a professional level and leaving out everything else.

I won't bullshit you and tell you it's a walk in the park, especially if there are people who were aware that you were involved, or even worse, nobody knows that you were involved so they have no appreciation for what you may be going through and so inadvertently end up hurting you with seemingly innocuous comments. The alternative to not doing NC is continuing to do the same thing and expecting a different result while potentially undermining your work performance, credibility or even your business. It's hoping that they will 'do the right thing' and prioritising your ego (and possibly your 'principles') and emotions over your wellbeing. If you don't do NC, you could end up losing your job or end up having to leave. *That's* more of a reality than NC not working.

I've also heard too many stories of awful disciplinary and mediation sessions in workplaces where attempts to continue engaging can end up being used against you by the other party. It is going to be hard (but not as hard as you think or as hard as continuing without NC) but it passes, especially if you keep busy, work hard and remain focused on your own personal growth and professional behaviour.

Make the Decision and Get On With It

This is a straight-up cold turkey situation. There are people out there who have so much self-control that they can do moderation, so for instance, they can eat naughty foods all of the time and not overdo it, but that's not the case for a lot of us and the truth is, if you could moderate your own behaviour with them while continuing to engage, you wouldn't be reading this book.

Be Professional

This is your job and your career and if you're planning to stick around, there will be far greater prices to pay than the pain you are going through now if you either behave in an unprofessional manner or allow what has happened to derail you. And this is coming from someone who at one point wanted to reach across my desk and throttle my ex. If you can afford not to give a monkey's about your job and your professionalism, you have to ask yourself why you're still there as you could leave and take yourself out of the pain zone. If you're going to remain in your role, it's time to pull it together.

We all have to work with people who get on our last nerve and who we don't like for certain reasons but we don't go in there and lose our shit with them each day or tell them all about themselves – it's the same when you break up. Yes you may have certain opinions but the fact that you work together precludes you from making them known verbally or via your actions. If you want to do that outside of work (pre-NC), then knock yourself out but always consider whether sounding off is going to do anything for your work situation or whether it's just to give you a quick high.

You can be professional and even friendly *without* being friends or pulling down your pants or starting a big discussion about your relationship.

It's quite a shift to go from bed partners to cordial, polite but distant, but it is extremely possible and judging by the amount of people who say that they have dalliances with people at work, there are a lot of people who have to get over someone they worked with and grin and bear it. And actually, it's the grinning and bearing it that helps; I don't mean grinning at them like a loon, but not taking the situation too seriously and pushing yourself through the awkwardness. Yes you may have to fake detachment when you really want to hurl yourself at them and beg for mercy, but don't. The litmus test of what you say and do is: would you say this to another work colleague? Yep, probably not.

Don't Resign Your Power

Don't be helpless and resign yourself to breaking contact before it's even started. Part of the reason why I initially struggled to end things is because I decided it would be:

1) Impossible to end it because we worked together – obviously that is not the case.

2) Too hard to be polite because I'd seem like a bitch or it might create tension – actually more tension was created by trying to do things on his terms and sacrificing my own needs.

3) I imagined what might happen if he asked me to meet up or told me he loved me still etc, and imagined being helpless to his advances – I *decided* that I had to be strong and that I wouldn't be helpless.

4) I couldn't imagine how we would both deal with clients we shared – well of course I couldn't imagine it. I hadn't actually tried to and had never experienced it before but I realised that I had to get on with it and do my job, because staying in a bad situation for a piddling little client, or even a big one, was not an option.

It's very easy to write off NC and make all sorts of excuses as to why it

The fact that they're charming or do 'cute' stuff doesn't disguise what they've clearly stated or shown, or even how you've been affected. You have to change your mindset because you'll sound like somebody who is expecting to break NC instead of someone who is planning for it to be a success because they're focused on themselves and rebuilding their life. *Don't think, "How can I stay strong?"* or *"I hope I will find the strength to be strong"* and instead think, *"I will stay strong"*. Repeat it frequently and do a bit of faking it till you feel it.

Avoid Discussing NC

If you've broken up before or claimed to be going NC, they'll just think that you're playing games. The best time to say something *if* you really have to, is if they approach you about the change in your behaviour. Don't say "I'm No Contact" and instead just explain briefly that you're fine, that you're taking the space that you need and that *of course* it won't stop you from being professional and then smile (if possible) and move away. Don't hang around for a discussion/validation and just head back to your desk or to the bathroom if you're feeling shaky.

Work Out What You Need To Do

NC is at its most successful when you do a bit of constructive thinking ahead and familiarise yourself with the typical routine between you both. Get a piece of paper and write down when and how they are most likely to get in touch and what it's about. If you know what their modus operandi is, you know what to expect, so you can plan ahead and build enough resolve to be ready should they attempt to make contact or you can just neutralise the effects of those cues and triggers by going through the grieving process and addressing any personal issues.

When they've typically engaged with you beyond the professional, how do they do it and how do you respond? This is where you get to identify cues, triggers and alternative responses. For instance, my ex assumed that when he wanted to go for lunch with me, that even if I was 'in a sulk', that I would say yes. The first time I declined, I'm sure he thought that it was a one-off but I kept declining. Whatever you would normally do outside of being professional, *stop* doing it.

In social situations, I made myself scarce by busying myself elsewhere talking to another group of people, and in some circumstances I left early. I didn't need to prove a point to myself, or take the high road and feel that I had every right to be there and that I shouldn't let him ruin my evening. This was more about how I didn't want to ruin my own evening by putting myself in the front line of pain. I only had to do it a couple of times and he got the message loud and clear and I didn't have to recover from any major blowups.

Easy On the Ruminating and Obsessing

You'll likely worry about what they think, what everyone else thinks, what they're doing, whether they're trying to screw up your job, why they're not chasing you, how not to cause a scene, how not to cry every time you come face to face, and you'll probably want to scream and yell at yourself for ever getting involved with a colleague. I've done it all. Sometimes I just wanted to throw myself on the floor and have an *I Can't Take Anymore Effing Thinking Tantrum*.

Worrying about what they or others are thinking is natural, especially in the first few weeks or so, but you'll be thinking *too* much about these things if you are still obsessing over these things months down the line and bringing your life, and possibly your career to a standstill. The obsessing will be about trying to work out what is going on in other people's minds and the likelihood is that you will end up doing things in an attempt to prevent unfavourable outcomes and manage your reputation. Unfortunately, you will just make the situation worse.

If you get behind your own decision, while you will have moments where you panic about what they or others think, it will always come back to meeting your *own* needs and the fact that your colleagues don't know and weren't in your situation so it's none of their business. Of course it *is* their business if you let your involvement play out around them or it affects your work performance, so keep it together.

This Is a Good Time to Be On a Bullshit Diet

Bad enough that you may have illusions in other circumstances but it's time to take off the blinders and get real if you're working together. Particularly if you feel a strong sense of rejection, it's important to remind yourself that just because they may be liked by their peers, they treat these people very well, they're highly respected, or they make a fortune or whatever, it *doesn't* distract from or change the fact that things did not work out with you. The way that somebody behaves at work and to 'their public' hasn't got a damn thing to do with how they behave behind closed doors. Don't make the mistake of persecuting yourself with the bullshit that comes about from imagining that someone has customised their persona *especially* for you. You know this person in a different way to everyone else.

Don't allow any perceived rejection to distort your sense of reality because many of you in this situation will convince yourself that everyone is talking about you or that you've been humiliated. You'd be surprised how many people will actually empathise with you – they may see this person for who they are and not actually be anywhere near as admiring as *you* are. This doesn't mean going and talking to them about it though, as you should be as professional as possible.

Give It Time

Work is a very routine place. Unless you're doing something chaotic, there's a hell of a lot of routine to your working week, which means that in adapting your routine and switching to professional, what seemed impossible will quickly become normal if you stick at it. If you don't have to speak to each other, don't. You also don't have to use any of the facilities at the same time, and if you do, don't engage. If you find yourself in the lift, in the kitchen making tea, or bumping into them in the corridor, smile and be polite. Practise smiling even when you're hurting, in front of the mirror. It'll stop you from looking 'manic' when you actually have to do it, but you'll also learn how to fake it till you feel it and probably have a giggle. Try to plan stuff at lunchtime or after work so that you have healthy distractions.

Avoid Gossip

Tempting as it may be to get the down low, you're opening yourself up to pain as you may learn far too much plus people chat a lot of rubbish anyway and add their own conjecture. Do you really want to know that he's trying for a baby with his wife? Or do you need to know that she's now trying to date someone in a different department?

- The upside of any info that you do catch is that it may cement your reason for doing NC.
- The downside is that you may magnify the meaning of this info, internalise it, give yourself a hard time, lose perspective and *react* to it.

Be very careful, for instance, if you hear someone saying that they've been looking a bit sad recently and then assuming it must be because they miss you. You don't know this and they may also be missing you for the wrong reasons!

But They're My Boss!

Whilst it's tempting to remain stuck in your position, and I mean this from a relationship perspective, all of the same rules apply as if they were a colleague, it's just that you will have to keep assessing the situation and at some point, you may have to weigh up whether this is worth it. The reality is that if you've slept with your boss, on a deeper level you likely accepted when you went into this that if it didn't work out that you'd have to leave, or maybe you assumed that *because* they were your boss that it was bound to work out because it was such a 'big risk' to take. *They* may have assumed that if and when it didn't work out that you would leave so if they *are* being difficult, it's a passive aggressive or even aggressive move to get you to go.

Some people abuse their power and in wanting to be in control of everything around them, may not appreciate you not dancing to their beat any longer. This may mean that they give you a hard time, either making things difficult at work or making it difficult for you to back off, either by being mean to you or by chasing you harder.

There's no easy way around it. If they're decent enough and accept that it's over and that they can't give you what you want, they may take a hint at NC. Some people *do* have pride so when you decide that you want to distance yourself, they respect it. But some people don't. They may be trapped in their own feelings and just don't do loss of control very well. I'd like to say that this isn't your problem but if they're your boss, it is. I've known of some bosses to arrange a transfer to another department or you can try to do this with HR. If things are very tense, they may not comply though and while you can remind this person about being professional, it's a bit tricky when they own the company and even if you threaten to sue or even do sue, it will likely mean having to move on.

It's best to avoid a showdown if you've decided to stay. Stick to all of the guidelines above and keep a note of any and all abuses of power. You may find it useful to have a brief discussion about wanting to move beyond your involvement in a professional manner.

- ❖ *Don't* make any declarations of feelings.
- ❖ *Don't* say anything inappropriate that displays overfamiliarity and use this discussion as an opportunity to flush out their position.
- ❖ *Do* take them at their word until they show otherwise if they say that they're willing to put your involvement aside.
- ❖ *Do* start looking for another job and weighing up your legal options if they show their arse and make clear that they're going to make your life difficult or that it's only going to end on their say-so. If you need time to get organised, use tips from the *Get Out Plan* chapter.

But I'm Their Boss!

I'm going to assume that if you've gone to the trouble of reading this book then you're likely in over your head and wondering how to extricate yourself out of this situation. Some people in your position are ruthless and mercenary and would think nothing of wielding their power and doing whatever it takes to get this person away from them, *but* that's not only the cowardly way to deal with things, it's a tad illegal to say the least.

Depending on what type of work setup you're in – sole trader and they're a contractor, small company with a HR person, two person company, big company, partner, manager, director or whatever – this may feel very close to home and a threat to your business/livelihood/reputation and this in itself can blind you and cause you to do and say things that you may later come to regret.

As the boss or certainly the one in a more senior position, you do need to consider your overall legal obligations as an employer, or your contractual obligations as an employee, or even whatever has been agreed between you both in a contract. The best thing to do, which is not always the *easy* thing to do, is to keep everything above board because trying to pay someone off under the table, making their life difficult or asking them to look for another role could get you into hot water. Sure they might be the type of person who goes "OK then" and shuffles off with their tail between their legs, but most people won't and even if they do, not only might they still come back at a later point and rightfully pursue a complaint against you, but if you do something shady now in the way that you handle this, it just paves the way to more shadiness. It will catch up with you because when you stop caring about your integrity, you will get caught out.

Here's the fundamental reason why NC situations can arise for a boss: nobody wants to feel discarded and when this is combined with the fact that some people find disappointment and rejection really tough to deal with never mind having to *work* for the person, this situation can activate a person's deepest fears and insecurities, and even affect their mental health.

You, regardless of how you may feel at this particular moment in time, are in the position of power and it may appear to the other party that there's less at stake for you or that you're 'getting away' with something, especially if this situation is the result of an affair. However you have come to be in this situation, this is a good time to have a very honest conversation with yourself and consider what you truly thought was going to happen here. *Did* you think about the possibility of this ending? *Did* you secretly assume that they would just leave if it didn't work out? *Did* you underestimate their feelings or overestimate your own or your capacity? *Have* you handled this situation poorly?

It's easy in this situation for the other party to feel like they're not being treated like a human with feelings and are just 'expected' to go back to the way things used to be and equally it's easy for you to end up feeling like The Bad Guy and at the same time genuinely afraid for your future. The best thing you can do here is *empathise*. It's not about ignoring your own feelings but it *is* about putting them aside long enough to imagine what this person might be thinking or feeling in *their* position. How would you feel if you were them? What would you do? Based on what you know of this person, is their reaction different to how you would deal with things and if so, why? Understanding things from *their* perspective instead of primarily seeing it from your own will help you to understand how this situation has blown up and possibly offer a path to finding a resolution. There's no easy way to deal with this situation so here's the bottom line:

- ❖ Ultimately this situation involves an element of compromise – finding a solution that you can both live with.

- ❖ If you have a discussion and are willing to set the terms of working together, as long as you're both respecting them, you should each be able to move on even if when you get home you have to vent your frustrations.

- ❖ If it's appropriate to your situation, consider a transfer to another department. Before you go suggesting this to your ex, I *would* ensure that what you're suggesting is above board.

- ❖ Don't inflame the situation. I'm not suggesting that you don't get on with your life but parading a new partner around who incidentally, may be another co-worker (not *again!*) is understandably inflammatory, hurtful and yes, disrespectful.

- ❖ Don't tell lies, especially ones that you're not only likely to be found out about but in persisting with the lie, you're actually crazy-making. Nobody likes being mind fucked. Yes I'm sure it's going to piss this person off if you admit that you've moved on or that you did whatever it is that they've found out about, but denying it is what can contribute greatly to destabilising a person and causing them to feel as if they're being talked about or being made a fool of.

- ❖ The shittier an exit you make out of this involvement, the less likely this will be to 'go away' so if you want to have a cat's hope in hell of this calming down and you both moving on from it, muster up all of the patience and courage you have and try to sit down and have a calm discussion.

- ❖ Choose a role – boss or friend. Bearing in mind the situation, you can't be both so don't keep trying to push a friend agenda to soothe your ego. Yes they might think you're an asshole right now but that's nothing compared to what they will think of you if you keep saying and doing things to make you look better while actually sending mixed messages and messing with this person's head.

❖ If you have an HR person, mentor or legal advisor, I would bite the bullet and have a conversation about how best to handle things. Many people in your situation try to save face and not tell anybody and end up creating more problems when in actual fact, speaking to these people and possibly arranging for discussion/mediation will communicate to the other party that you're serious and that you're going to address this issue.

❖ If you're an employee, you may be obliged by contract to admit your involvement which is tricky as there may be serious consequences for doing so. That said, explaining to this person that you are willing, or going, to speak to HR may 'sober' them up. That said, if you're dealing with someone who doesn't give a shit or is eager for the company to know so that you can get into trouble, *that's* a problem.

❖ That said, you are as much a party to this involvement as they were so don't attempt to smear their reputation. Be responsible and accountable for your involvement.

❖ Don't try to use sex, lunches, gifts, promises of a promotion etc, to butter them up because it's no wonder you're struggling to end this – you're sending mixed messages and *kinda* buying their silence.

❖ If this is a crush, flirtation or one-nighter gone awry, be firm (avoid being cruel) in saying that a line is being drawn under the situation and remain absolutely professional because the fact that you have to do NC in this situation suggests something that shouldn't have gotten out of hand, *has*. It may help to say, "I apologise for my part in this situation arising and moving forward

I just want to assure you that I'll keep a polite and professional distance."

❖ If you treat this person in the way that you treat other staff members (which is hopefully decently), you at least don't have to worry about discrimination.

❖ Be careful of what you say such as, "If it wasn't for the fact that we're working together then…" because if this isn't true and then this person goes "OK then, I've left my job/got transferred to a different department", you're going to be in a very tight spot. Again.

****

Ultimately, whatever your feelings are, work is work, and some companies seriously frown upon your professionalism and ability to do your role being impeded by sexual relationships. Should they attempt to cross the line with you, don't be afraid to remind them that this is your place of work. Harsh as it may sound, for the ones that persist at trying to contact you, keep a note of everything – you never know if you may need to use it. Also remember that if you remain professional, *they* don't have anything that they can be keeping a note of about *you*.

MONEY MONEY MONEY MONEY MONEY... *MONEY*!

Money is something that has broken relationships of all kinds and is a very sensitive subject and it can be super-awkward when a romantic relationship breaks down. At this juncture, it's too late to be asking how they came to be borrowing money from you or even how *you* came to be borrowing it and to be fair, the way the economy is these days, it's unsurprising that we may find ourselves having to lend a financial helping hand or even being the borrower. I won't lie when I say that you're in a bit of a conundrum if you want to go NC and there's the not-so-small matter of money.

When You Owe Money

There's nothing wrong with you needing to go NC but before you go down this road, address the money situation otherwise it will look like you're doing a bunk in order to avoid paying back the money which will in turn invite this person into your life. It's better for you to take the bull by the horns and propose a solution for paying them back if you can't pay it back in full now, or pay them back straight away even if you have to eat baked beans for a week. An ex, especially a toxic one who thinks that they have free reign to abuse you because you owe them money is not worth the aggravation.

❖ If you said that you were going to pay it back, follow through on your word.

- ❖ If you didn't think that they'd ask for it back but it was understood to be a loan at the time, you still have to pay it back.

- ❖ If they haven't asked for the money and you think it's likely they will or you just want to square things off, pay it back.

- ❖ If your circumstances have changed and they affect the original agreement that you made, this is the time to let them know that you can't meet the original agreement but that you will in _____ and then let them know when and how it will be paid back (in full or in installments).

- ❖ If terms of payment haven't been agreed and it's a big enough amount that you'd prefer not to pay in full now, take the initiative and send an email or a letter, or yes, even pick up the phone and let them know the number of instalments, the amount, and set up a standing order.

- ❖ If there's someone else that you'd rather be in debt to, borrow the money from them and then pay your ex back. And then go about your NC business.

- ❖ Taking control of the situation and paying back/making the appropriate arrangements is better than trying to stay in contact to keep them off your back or to avoid paying back the money while being miserable.

- ❖ Don't pretend that the money situation doesn't exist and still attempt to proceed with NC because unless you have little conscience, it's likely going to cause anxiety.

- ❖ If you genuinely believe that you don't owe the money ("It was a gift!") or that you don't owe as much as they say, you will need to have a discussion about it. Admittedly face-to-face or over the phone is quicker simply because you could end up playing email tennis. If the amount is large enough (or they're petty), you could end up being taken to court so make sure you have any and all correspondence relating to this money.

❖ Do seek legal advice (the Citizens Advice Bureau in the UK for instance) if needed or consider working with a mediator. The latter will demonstrate that you're more than willing to get the situation ironed out although it's likely to have a cost attached to it. Plus whoever you consult is likely to convey to your ex that the route they're pursuing is costly and/or futile (if appropriate).

When They Owe You Money

Depending on what type of person you've been involved with – if they're high up on the shady scale or even just vaguely manipulative – they will put your desire for that money and the fact that they don't have access to you together and *leverage* it. This means any personal power you're gaining by stepping back and going NC may be hugely affected by this person dangling money that you're rightfully owed.

It's hard to hear, but if you're serious about ending it, you have to contemplate the possibility of not getting some or all of the money. It's a pain in the bum but as I've learned from personal experience, if I could lend it, I could afford to lose it and the cost of pursuing this debt, especially emotionally and mentally, may be too expensive. I have an ex that still owes me over $2,000 and I could have done with that money at the time and I could still think of a few things I could spend it on right now. But in letting it go, I've experienced abundance in many other ways in the *twelve* years (at time of publishing) since I loaned him the money.

❖ Prepare for cutting contact by having a final conversation about the money *before* you go NC especially if there's no payback agreement in place because if you don't, they may assume that you're willing to write off the debt.

❖ Agree the terms, how much, when, if it's in full, if it's installments, how it's going to be paid etc.

❖ If you gave this person money and gifts as a means of, oh I don't know, buying their affections or compliance, it's not really fair to ask for the money. This is something that happens to many an over-giving people pleaser and when things don't work out, they feel 'wronged' and taken advantage of because they had quietly or even very openly assumed that all of this 'giving' would generate certain things. It's a hard lesson to learn but if it wasn't an agreed loan or there wasn't a clear agreement about what these 'gifts' were in exchange for, you need to cut your losses.

❖ Before getting to the point of worrying about *if* it will be paid back, clarify that they *know* that it's supposed to be paid back. You'd be surprised how many people will claim that they thought the money was a gift...

❖ If you've already agreed terms, don't assume that because you're ending things that they'll pay it back sooner – get confirmation, otherwise you'll need to suck it up and stick to the original agreement.

❖ Don't go in hostile – it doesn't make the person want to pay you back plus you're not in Lock, Stock and Two Smoking Barrels... Starting an argument will not bring out their best side. Also avoid coming across as petty, manipulative, or bitchy, even if you feel entitled to do so.

❖ Be calm, factual, and unemotional *especially* around somebody who knows how to play you like a finely tuned guitar.

❖ If it's face-to-face, rehearse what you're going to say and do consider how you will respond to any 'objections'. Have two options for getting the money back but just suggest your preferred one and save the other one as a backup because if you don't, they'll likely negotiate with your plan B.

❖ Make sure you clarify whether they're in a position to pay the money back and don't ever think about uttering the words 'Take your time' or 'Don't worry about paying me back immediately'. This people-pleasing behaviour is where you're busting your own boundaries. If they can take their time and they don't need to worry about it, why go there with this conversation?

❖ Don't make an agreement that involves you having to behave like a debt collector. Have them set up a standing order where the money is automatically debited from their account on the date you've both agreed. Paypal is also quick and easy for collecting money and in this day and age, there's no need for them to be doing this cheque bullshit or insisting on dropping around cash.

❖ Remember that the more complicated that you make the instructions for how you get the money, the more layers to your probable headache. "Well... I suppose you could put it in my bank account but then I'm thinking that it would be easier if you sent it wrapped up on the back of a donkey or put half in this account, a quarter off that bill account and the rest off this other bill..." Just put it in one account. Money can be moved. By you. When you get it paid back. Don't make things hard for yourself.

❖ It's easier to get all of this stuff in writing which is why email can be so useful. If this discussion happens over the phone, you can always follow it up with an email clarifying the key points. Also make sure that you ask them to confirm that they've set up the standing order.

❖ Don't change the terms. This is a lesson in respecting boundaries. I appreciate that sometimes circumstances change but if you've both made an agreement, it's a tad unfair to change the goalposts. Of course you may feel that you're in dire straits and it's understandable then to ask them but you may be putting them on the spot.

I know it's a pain in the ass, I know it's your money, but be careful that chasing your money doesn't suck you back into the relationship and cripple you emotionally.

What you do learn after this is not that there cannot be money in relationships, but that money is something that should never be a part of relationships that don't exist, barely exist, or already have a whole host of problems because mo' money, mo' problems and you're trying to plug a gaping hole in your relationship dam that cannot be filled.

LEGAL STUFF

If you have kids, a home, financial agreements, a business, you will need to consult with a professional – trust me it is a lot easier to do this now than to only start thinking about it when you're angry because they've moved on. I have friends who thought they were dealing with someone who while they were no longer together was being halfway decent – wait until they get a new partner and see how things change.

You get a better deal and less stress if you act now. Don't delay the inevitable.

❖ **Find out your legal rights and have a plan A and plan B.** For instance, I know a number of people who purchased homes together and then broke up. One wanted to stay in the house or wanted to avoid selling because even though they didn't want to step up in the relationship, they didn't want things to be final.

❖ **If for whatever reason you cannot sell the property, it's easier if you both move out and rent out the property.** If the rent amount allows for it, consider letting it be handled by a property management company. If not, have everything written down – my friend did a lot of it by email and it covered all bases.

❖ **If it's a joint financial agreement, you're both liable.** Remember that if you are on a joint mortgage and you privately agree for them to continue living there and paying it, if they default, you are liable for the payments. Consult a lawyer/solicitor/mediator and find out your rights and what you can do, including drawing up a legal agreement and consulting with your bank. Things change – it's better to future proof.

❖ **If you own a business together, I certainly wouldn't agree to selling your share or leaving without consulting with a solicitor/lawyer.** Make sure the business is properly valued and that you sit down and work out who has been doing what because being clear on who has brought value to the business may be needed to work things out. In the interim, get a written agreement in place about how things will be run. If you're both happy to dissolve the business, it should be outlined in the documents about how the dissolution affects the formation of future businesses.

❖ **Remove yourself from any bills that you're no longer responsible for.** Sure it might be 'inconvenient' for your ex to have to put their name on their own bills that they're paying but it takes a matter of minutes and you have your own home and bills to be worrying about.

❖ **Keep a record of every conversation, email, text, correspondence etc.** You will thank yourself further down the line.

❖ **Don't fear talking to a professional.** If each time you get into discussions it gets nasty or doesn't get anywhere, hire a mediator or other legal professional (see the chapter *Co-Parenting*). Sometimes just mentioning that you're going to do this is enough to get them to cooperate. Yes these things cost money but it's nothing compared to how much it can cost you if left unaddressed.

THE GET OUT PLAN

If you're working with this person, still living together, they're married/attached, you have practical stuff to resolve, or they're just exceptionally hard of hearing and possibly abusive, you may feel that it's going to be very problematic if you do straight up NC or even LC. It may also be for yourself, in that you may feel that you need to gradually build up to going full NC – to do this, you need a *Get Out Plan*.

A **Get Out Plan** is a carefully coordinated effort where you start to **ease out of the relationship in preparation for cutting off contact.** It's ideal if there are things you need to tie up before you go, you've fallen off the wagon before, or you need to do NC with a particularly aggressive person who will pursue you intensely or even be very difficult with you if you don't do things on their terms – i.e. the extra controlling types that want to know where you're at every hour of the day, are accusing you of being with someone else, and who like to treat you badly or dump you and then feign bewilderment at your upset. A Get Out Plan **gives you time to get yourself emotionally, mentally, physically and even spiritually prepared** rather than jerking out of the relationship and panicking at your reaction to it. This is why they're particularly effective when you can't see past the short term or you tend to second-guess yourself. Get Out Plans are also perfect for flip-flappers (you or them), because it's a bit like weaning yourself gradually off cigarettes or drugs. When you make the final leap, it won't feel like so much of a leap.

There are two big glaring questions though that you need to ask yourself before implementing this plan:

1) Do you really want to end the relationship or are you looking for another means of buying time to provide the opportunity to stay invested and attempt to change this person?
*2) How much worse do you need to be treated or how much more drama do you want to engage in before it's **enough**?*

If you're not sure if you want to break up, a Get Out Plan may not be for you. However be careful of being sucked into more drama or being mistreated further. There *has* to be a cut-off point. When you begin to step back, you'll find that you gain objectivity and perspective so that in turn the genuine desire to make and stick to the break becomes very real.

Set A Deadline

Not a pretend one that you'll move to buy more time in a few weeks or months, but a real deadline. Make it challenging but realistic – don't make it so long it's a joke, but don't make it so short that you're going to panic and reschedule. Nothing longer than six months to a year though (for longer term relationships) and preferably it should be 1 to 3 months. While of course you could shoot for a three-year plan for instance, the Get Out Plan is really about a concentrated effort to get out and the longer it is, the more likely it is that you will deviate off course. The deadline is really about preparation including finances, legalities etc, because the truth is, relying solely on being emotionally ready means you'll never be ready, not least because you need to focus on the actions and habits to strengthen that willingness to go and to bolster you emotionally.

If your ex or soon-to-be ex is abusive, be careful of wavering just because there's been a good day or week – this isn't the only good day or week you've had and it doesn't excuse their previous actions nor is having a good day or week a sign that a very big problem has been magically 'fixed'. You have to base your plans on reality not on this hope that they'll change and you'll be spared from having to do anything.

Or, Choose the Next Big Thing

Some people find setting a date quite difficult and in this case, go with The Next Big (Shitty) Thing that happens. Only thing is that it could happen tomorrow or next week. We often have an idea though of the type of stunts that they may pull or of our own personal levels of upset, so you can base it on this. I vowed that the next time that he picked an argument with me or that I felt insignificant, I was out. Don't budge from your agreement with yourself as this will create distrust and undermine what little confidence you have left.

Confide In Someone

It's widely acknowledged that telling people about goals and plans is a good motivator due to the sense of accountability that arises. It's tempting to keep it a secret because if you change your mind, nobody will know about it and it won't matter as much about what you're sticking around for. When it comes to NC, if you're trapped in your feelings and also keeping your own experience and pain a secret, you won't sanity check your decisions and get the support that you need. Tell a trusted friend, family member or even co-worker your deadline so that you stick to it. The alternative is to speak to a counsellor, therapist, or join a local support group – you are not alone in your circumstances.

It's particularly important that you confide in someone if you're in an abusive relationship. There's often this worry that you'll be judged or that no one will believe you when actually, this is rarely the case. Many victims of abuse have found it incredibly helpful to talk to a co-worker, possibly because attempting to see a professional for instance, might have alerted suspicion whereas a co-worker won't come under suspicion.

Slowly Start Adapting Your Habits

This is the key to it all – you need to begin to gradually withdraw and adapt your routine. Not only does distance give you objectivity so that you start to see this person, yourself, and the relationship in a more realistic light, but it means that by the time you end it, the cold turkey is not going to be as bad as wrenching yourself out of habits. What does this involve?

SAY YES LESS

This is a good time to spend a week or so just paying attention to what you typically say or show yes to on a day-to-day basis. You may be surprised to discover how little you say no and how often you're silencing your own needs, expectations and wishes in favour of saying what you think people want to hear due to fear of conflict. Saying yes all the time *isn't* going to get you out of this relationship *nor* is it going to lead to an even moderately healthy relationship with anyone, romantic or otherwise.

Make other plans at times when they're likely to expect you to be available. It's quite liberating to say no instead of saying yes as a default and feeling taken advantage of. Even if you don't make plans and end up staying home, don't accept every invitation to go out. If you have a three-month plan, start dropping a meetup a week and then drop another one – in essence, reduce the amount of time you spend together.

Rather than shock the crap out of yourself and others by suddenly saying no to everything, gradually build up your assertive muscles. Start with the small stuff and gradually build up from there.

STOP TAKING EVERY CALL

Many drama-filled relationships have people who answer every single call and are basically available on tap. Stop it. Let's say you speak 5 times a day normally, drop to 4, then 3, and so on. They're likely to get angry or irritated, or even blow hot when you do this but pay no attention. Don't explain that you're reducing your calls – just say that you're busy with work, a friend, whatever – make something up if you have to! In fact, line them up for the reduced calls by feeding them a story about your increased workload. Unplug your house phone if they're the type to start calling this if they don't get you on your mobile/cell.

DELAY REPLIES TO EMAILS AND TEXTS

Whatever your normal response time is, double it or triple it, or even don't bother to respond. One of the best ways is if they send a text the night before, reply back in the morning. Even if you did nothing other than twiddle your thumbs, you look busy.

CUT LATE NIGHT CALLS

Most smartphones also have a 'Do not disturb' setting so it can automatically stop giving you notifications or ringing after a certain time.

STOP ENGAGING

As you gradually distance yourself, they may react to the sudden change and pick a fight or question you about your actions. Do. Not. Engage. Certainly don't explain. It will totally catch them off guard. All those things that you would normally throw a wobbly about and create a whole load of drama – don't. Sit on your hands, tape your mouth, run out of the house, do whatever you need to do, but bite your tongue and play nice.

PAY CLOSER ATTENTION

Instead of taking what they say at face value or being suckered in by lust, watch their actions more closely, listen keenly to what they say and observe the changes in your own behaviour around them as well as observing the impact on the overall dynamic. If it helps, keep a Feelings Diary, which is basically noting your moods and the shifts in them. They are great for identifying your cues, triggers and typical responses. There's a Feelings Diary worksheet available from my site. http://bit.ly/ncfdbkk

EASE UP ON THE SEX

I'm all for getting laid but sex clouds judgement and puts you in the Justifying Zone, that special place we go to when we continue investing because we're sexually/emotionally invested and don't want to believe that we've made a poor judgment. All of those happy hormones flying around may convince you that the huge orgasm is a reason to stick around. Naturally by seeing them less, there are less opportunities to be seduced.

BE CAREFUL OF ALCOHOL

If getting a bit tipsy or drunk fuels some of your drama or passion, it's time to cut back so that you don't get derailed.

HAVE MORE PERSONAL AND SOCIAL TIME

Learning to love yourself and spending time alone is one of the best things that can happen, not only because loving yourself makes you very self-aware of people who negate or hamper it, but it also means that when you cut contact, you will feel like an entity as opposed to feeling like you've been robbed and left with nothing because your relationship has ended.

Create your own life with meaning and embrace family and friends, or take part in activities that help you to meet new people.

If these relationships have suffered during your involvement, do use some of this time to begin repairing these relationships. Don't isolate yourself and even though it can hurt to admit where you've erred, admitting it will stop you from isolating yourself in this relationship. If you really don't feel that you can return to these relationships, do look at attending a local support group – check out Meetup.com.

****

You may find that you start NC in full before you reach your deadline because the great thing about withdrawing is that you see them as they are and you also recognise how much better you feel by not being drawn into the cycle. I once had a reader tell me she was giving herself three months on her plan and it took her only two weeks because the shift in her own behaviour made her realise how ridiculous he was and she went full NC and ended it.

Listen to yourself while doing the Get Out Plan. Note what stresses you out, note where you feel panicked and also note when you feel good and why.

When you become distracted from the end goal of going to full NC, evaluate what you're afraid of, whether it's fear about something that is actually happening or whether it's irrational fear that isn't being sanity checked against what you know of your experiences with this person. If there are areas that you're struggling with that you feel that you need advice on, use local resources as well as the internet to focus on finding solutions – this could be legal services, support groups, therapists, counsellors, the police, or specialists in a particular area, for instance if you know that this person may be difficult due to an addiction.

It's important to use this time to be committed to your plan and to *get* committed to making the jump. Keep validating what you're doing along the way by reminding yourself of why you're making this decision. You *can* do this.

FANTASY RECOVERY

People can feel quite helpless after a fantasy relationship has to come to an end because it feels as if they don't have options for recovery due to it not being 'real'. Actually, recovering from a crush, virtual relationship or even a dalliance that didn't quite make it to a date meeting up can be quite devastating if you had a lot of hopes and expectations tied up in it and you were fantasising due to feelings of inadequacy that have been exacerbated by the fallout.

Time For a Fantasy Holiday

Tempting as it may be to avoid your feelings by finding someone new to fixate on, this is part of the reason why you're in these problems in the first place. All you're doing is a reset and... lather, rinse, repeat.

Keep a Feelings Diary

This is to keep you grounded, accountable and aware of your feelings and urges. Get to understand where you're losing chunks of time on daydreaming or even giving yourself a hard time. Evaluate when you tend to feel most rejected – what is happening at that time, how you are feeling, what you are afraid of etc. Grab the worksheet - http://bit.ly/ncfdbkk

Be Accountable and Responsible

This is a toughie to face but the fact is, if you don't like where you are right now, you cannot put it all on the other person. This was your crush, your fantasy, your hopes and expectations and so while it's understandable to feel disappointed that it didn't come to pass as you would like, you cannot be angry with the other party for not meeting hopes and expectations that weren't directly communicated. This is a good time to *listen* to what these hopes and expectations were and look at how you can cultivate these in your own life. Acknowledge that you have needs but *recognise* that if you don't meet them in reality, they're certainly not going to be happening in a fantasy.

Hold That Thought

When you're tempted to confront them or fire off an email, delay doing anything for at least 24 hours no matter how tempting it is. I guarantee you that if you do anything off the back of your feelings, you will then not only be hurting from it not working out but will then have to deal with feelings of regret and embarrassment.

Daydream In Time Slots

Set allocated time slots of 15 minute daydream breaks in the morning, afternoon and evening. Outside of these times, force yourself to focus on something else. That means when at work you have to think about work or something else. Learn to recognise the signs of when your mind is drifting and do the equivalent of mentally pulling over on the side of the road after falling asleep at the wheel. You wake yourself up and you pull your mind back to the present.

Don't keep revisiting the so-called 'rejection'

It's the equivalent of repeatedly returning to your pain or in the crudest terms, going back to look at your own vomit. That's a pretty damn unpleasant image but it's even more unpleasant to relive the rejection over and over again. This is persecution. You don't deserve this.

Grieve All Of Your Losses

Sounds daunting but it's a must. When you have fantasy involvements, it's likely that you are carrying several suitcases of hurt from crush to crush or involvement to involvement. When each fantasy ends, it reopens the old wounds which you try to escape in a new crush or by going back to your pain source. Read the section on loss.

Brainstorm How To Nurture Yourself

Spend some time coming up with several ways in which you could treat yourself with love, care, trust and respect. Fantasy involvements and giving yourself a hard time from rejection stem from low self-esteem and avoiding intimacy. You are loving and admiring from a distance in order to limit how close someone can get to you. You enjoy the feelings of the fantasy more than putting yourself out there but it's stopping you from enjoy life in reality. You're hiding from yourself and you're hiding from intimacy and the world. Whatever it is that is stopping you from loving yourself, it's time to address it. If this has been a longstanding habit or you find the process of putting your feet firmly in reality quite daunting, don't be afraid to seek additional support.

DEALING WITH THREATS

Sometimes a person becomes desperate when they feel out of control and they use something that they either already know works, or they try it for the first time, and due to the way in which you respond, they continue to employ these means of controlling your agenda – threats. Whether they're threatening to injure themselves or you, or to cause some form of retribution, what you cannot do is make yourself responsible for this person. If you do, next thing you know, you'll still be in this situation due to fear, guilt, pity or all of these, none of which are conducive to a healthy relationship.

Threats do a 'wonderful' job of scaring you into compliance *especially* if you're already someone who tends to be a fixer/healer/helper who tries to right the wrongs of the past and even more so if you're a blame absorber.

There's no easy way to deal with threats of suicide or self-harm. What I can tell you is that I've heard from hundreds of people who are NC who have felt panicked by an ex's claims of being on the verge of doing something. These people have either felt gravely concerned due to the history of this person's behaviour or have been frightened due to it seeming out of character. It's easy to put two and two together and draw the conclusion that NC has caused your ex serious mental and emotional harm.

Unfortunately what tends to happen is that regardless of whether it's a regular thing or it comes out of the blue, most respond and then discover that the person was far from serious and even claims to have 'forgotten' about the incident, or even worse, claims that the worried ex is being 'melodramatic'. Of course there's always the chance that this person is serious but nonetheless, you have to carefully consider what you do next because regardless of the threats, what *isn't* an option is opting back into the dynamic in an attempt to stave off the possibility. It immediately renders this relationship an incredibly unhealthy and codependent one. What you do next will help *both* of you and/or make clear that you cannot be manipulated.

Ultimately, whether they're threatening to harm themselves or you, what you cannot do is go back and hold yourself hostage to this situation.

❖ If you genuinely believe that their threats of suicide or self-harm are serious and imminent, call the emergency services. While you may believe that you're equipped to handle this situation, you're not. Even if you could calm them down, you're ignoring what these threats represent – issues that need handling by *this* person and a professional. By attempting to make you the solution to their problem, you could put yourself in danger, plus you're obstructing their need and responsibility to get help.

❖ If you do decide to go and see them, be prepared that it may not be the situation that's been portrayed. It's upsetting, but just be relieved and go home.

❖ If this has previously happened, it may be best to get in touch with a family member or friend of theirs. This is tricky because the one making the threats may not react very well to you doing this but it's their threat that's put you between a rock and a hard place and they have no right to place that responsibility on you.

❖ If they're threatening to harm you or your property or even your family and friends, don't disregard the threat and do report them. *Especially* if there's a history of abuse in the relationship *or* you are aware of previous complaints/convictions for stalking and abusive behaviour. Don't try to be the exception to the rule and certainly don't downplay their threats because the first time you might realise that they're serious might be when it's too late. Keep a record of everything and speak with your local law enforcement – you would be surprised what you may discover when you make the report as it's very possible that you're not the first.

❖ If you're scared to leave your home or are experiencing a great deal of anxiety about the threats, do apply for a restraining order. Sometimes it's the wake-up call that a person needs. Don't violate this order yourself though as it undermines it, plus respecting the order is pivotal in helping abuse to be taken seriously. Violating it may also inadvertently give leverage to your ex who could twist this whole thing around.

❖ It's not about you; it's displacement of their feelings and thoughts. Yes you have been NC and they have to deal with what that loss represents, which may in turn bring up some very uncomfortable feelings from previous experiences. It's understandable to check up on them but what you cannot do is restart the relationship or attempt to 'save' them or control their threatening behaviour – you're not *that* powerful. It's also important to remember that you're not committing a wrongdoing by ending the relationship or maintaining a distance. If anything, the fact that these threats are happening underscores how much this decision was and is needed. This is a highly toxic situation. You do *not* deserve this treatment irrespective of whatever happened in the relationship.

❖ Don't deal with these threats alone. You have nothing to be ashamed of and keeping these threats a secret is isolating. Talk to friends and family and don't be afraid to seek professional help because situations like this are traumatic. Talking about this and seeking help will help you to gain some much-needed perspective.

❖ If this situation is similar to another event from the past or this person's behaviour is bringing up an old wound, such as not being able to stop a parent from doing something destructive or being blamed for their boundary violations, it's pivotal to differentiate between these two sets of experiences so that you don't end up trying to right the wrongs of the past. Seeking professional support can also help to lay the old traumas to rest.

❖ If you allow this person's threats to run your life, you'll gradually feel like you have no life left. Intimidation and guilt is not love.

CUTTING OFF A NARCISSIST

If you're serious about No Contact and you've been dealing with a narcissist or you suspect them to be due to abusive behaviour, it's really important that you put your own ego aside (ironic I know) and truly heed what I'm going to say in this chapter. If you don't, the pain that you will experience further down the line is nothing compared to what you may be in now or previously.

What is absolutely critical to recognise here is that it doesn't matter if they're a diagnosed narcissist (or sociopath/psychopath) or whether you *suspect* them to be – the fact that you would suspect someone of this issue speaks volumes about what you've been experiencing. What I wouldn't do is attempt to be the exception to a rule that no one else has managed to be the exception to – narcissists don't love and the way that their minds operate is very different to a human with empathy. Sure, I suppose if you want to look at the possibility of this person loving you, behaving themselves and basically no longer having this personality disorder as your fairy tale, I can see why you might think that getting this person to do these things would represent an incredibly 'valuable' love but that's like saying that you'd rather spend your life trying to get water from an empty well and getting high off the occasional drip.

NC All The Way – No Exceptions

You cannot do partial contact with a narcissist and attempt to be their mate and certainly not with someone who has been abusive and/or exploitative.

Any interaction by you is just coins in their ever filling attention jar. They don't do nuances so while you may feel like you have a logical reason for responding or even reaching out to them, they just think "They love me."

If you've done your reading up on narcissism or even sociopaths, you'll know that NC is the only way to get your life back. You can be food in their cage for them to feed off of, or you can cold turkey it and focus on addressing why you were involved with them in the first place. They won't like you cutting it off and feeling like they've lost and are not in control – tough shit – and it's important for you to not lose sight of this. You haven't liked being on the receiving end of their treatment either and the difference is, you don't have a personality disorder so you need to stop trying to fight against this and stop acting like you're coming from the same perspective. Narcissists like to abandon you first before you have the good sense to see them for what they are and get away from them. You cutting off will get on their nerves (and then some) but they will only woo you back and bait and goad you so that they can put you in a position where they can abandon you.

Don't Remind Them To Stop Contacting You

Even responding to say that you don't want them to contact you or reminding them why is not only contact but it's also more coins in their attention jar. They will bait and goad and bait and goad until they get the response that they want. Unless they're of the stalking/dangerous variety, they will eventually move on to a new target while likely trying to reach out to you again. Do not respond. Make it easier for yourself by blocking as many forms of contact as you can so that you don't even see it. Then they can get their attention rocks off on their own time.

They will not like you not giving attention as if your 'role' and goal in life is to be some sort of attention slave. That's how they see people. They may very well be pissed off but just remember, **the only reason they are getting in touch is to put you back in that role.** They don't do feelings and they don't do empathy so they have not changed and if you fall for this, you will find yourself in a hell of a lot of pain and will feel duped when their charm wears off.

Stop Trying To Outthink Them

Stop concerning yourself with what the next move might be. Unless you're a narcissist or a sociopath yourself, you really will have no idea what is running through their mind. If you want to know what to expect, plot out your relationship on a chart, mark the highs, mark the lows, mark who got in touch with who, how long there has been between contacts, and how they typically respond to conflict, criticism, you saying NO, you asserting your needs, etc. *That's* what to expect.

Stop Justifying

Every time you have the urge to explain or engage or both, remember: there's no point; they cannot empathise. Think about the logic of this – narcissist or not, you believe this person to have empathy issues so why do you keep trying to explain your position or giving yourself a hard time for them not understanding your position and empathising with it? That just doesn't make sense. Don't engage with them. It's one thing if you want to stress out your brain from afar trying to figure out how someone can behave in this way or be so devoid of compassion and care, but do not try to do it *with* them. It's like trying to recover from a broken leg while putting it under a chainsaw.

Don't Be A Puppet

When you consider going back and engaging, think of yourself like a puppet – everything that you do with a narcissist is about them believing that they are tugging at your strings and having you fulfil your role in The

Great Narcissist at The Royal Assholery Theatre. Why go and play your part? If you think you can go to the 'play' and come up with your own role or start saying lines that don't fit with the role and the play, think again. They will squash you with a ferocity that can literally take your breath away.

Don't 'Fire Shots'

Do not tell them about themselves as some sort of parting shot. Don't. If you do, aside from the fact that they'll take it as a signal of more attention and feed off it while marking your cards as a psycho or something, depending on what flavour of aggressive they are, they can become verbally or even physically violent or do something to diminish your reputation. If they really are a narcissist or narcissistically inclined, then you should already know that you never tell them that they are, no matter how tempting; you walk, in fact *sprint*, away.

Don't Fall For The Apology Trick

Next thing you know, they'll be getting you to apologise which is an attempt to press the Reset Button in exchange for you being allowed back into the harem. **Do not apologise** – narcissists take it to mean that you're apologising for 'everything' including their actions. You may think that if you apologise that everything will be OK, but when they sink their proverbial teeth into you again, you'll regret thinking that you could treat them like a normal person with feelings.

Don't Publicise Your Pain

Another reason they get in touch or keep track of you is to ensure that you're miserable without them – it's another source of attention. If you message them back saying "Leave me alone! I'm in so much pain!" they don't feel guilty; they collect some money for the attention jar. Don't posts statuses on Facebook about how much your life is crumbling, don't look like you haven't slept or eaten in a month even if you haven't, and don't let anyone chat about your business to them. Don't tell them that you can't stop thinking about them or that you're nothing without them – er, how much of a frickin ego stroke can you give one person?

Attention in the form of your misery is attention and for a narcissist, that's all that matters and they don't actually need to be with you to get that attention. These people feel just as stoked with the knowledge that you're miserable without them. NC removes that knowledge.

Stop Scratching The Narcissistic Attention Itch

It may seem impossible now, but believe me – if you don't scratch the contact itch, over time, if you get on with your own life, that need to scratch it will fade. Each time you scratch the contact itch will set you back, especially as being with a narcissist is pretty damn traumatic. This person reminds you of someone from your past, likely your childhood in a big way. Address *that* so that you stop thinking that this person who may be great on a good day but *horrendous* on another is 'normal' and as good as it gets.

UNDERSTANDING THE DYNAMIC

NC BREAKS UNHEALTHY HABITS

Have you ever told someone that it's over or made threats and then found yourself backsliding and going back on your word? If you have a cycle of breaking up and getting back together, or staying even though you've said that you've had enough or that certain things have to change "or else", this has been contributing a lot to how much they believe, whether it's consciously or subconsciously, that they can get away with. The first time you shouted the modern day dating equivalent of 'WOLF!', they were probably scared.

"I can't take this anymore!"
"We're over!"
"Well piss off back to your ex then!"
"You pull this ever again and we're through! You got me?!"

But there is one thing that lets them know that you're crying wolf – you're *still* there, so when you say:

"I can't take this anymore!" They learn that actually, you *can* because you're always widening your yardstick to accommodate their behaviour.

"We're over!" They learn that it's an empty threat. It's over till you panic about who they're with, where they're at, who they're doing, and how you're ever going to resist/get over them.

"Well piss off back to your ex then!" They take you at your word and then

you hunt them down to come back and even take up the role of the Other Woman/Guy to keep them in your life at any cost. Or as soon as the words are out of your mouth, you apologise for saying it and even apologise for *their* behaviour!

"You pull this ever again and we're through! You got me?!" They do it again, and you stay and they know after that that they can pretty much do as they please. They also know that you're a ranter and a threatener but you're certainly not a mover and shaker. The first time you raised hell, they were scared. Maybe even the second, third, and tenth time. At some point, they realised that you were mostly talk and worked out the pattern of the dynamic between you both. Because you're still there, they think it's empty threats or at the very least, that you consider them your *best option*.

Crying wolf gives you the temporary illusion of a power shift. These situations are so frustrating that you can miss the memo that it has the hallmarks of a get-the-hell-out-of-dodge situation because you're too busy trying to get things on your terms and battling your own insecurities that are likely part of the reason you think that this person is as good as it gets.

If you're at this NC juncture, you've probably tried a variety of methods to get some movement in the relationship area of your life, and instead, have found yourself going round and round in a vicious circle. You just can't shake them or your need to keep going back to the relationship 'crime scene', and you keep saying how unhappy you are yet you keep revisiting the same situation. Crying 'wolf' is representative of there being an unhealthy dynamic between you both as well as the existence of unhealthy habits of thinking and behaviour that have you living off crumbs and essentially turning someone else's crumb into your overblown loaf while neglecting your own needs, wishes and expectations.

You've had or are approaching your 'enough moment' – that event or instance no matter how small that tips you over the edge and galvanises you into action. But... you know yourself and the reality is that if you trusted yourself and knew what to expect from yourself, you probably wouldn't be reading this.

Something brought you to this point and now you need to build upon it. In order to not only make NC successful but more importantly, change your relationship habits so that you can be happier and ultimately find a relationship more befitting of you, you need to understand how to break your pattern and why that pattern exists in the first place.

You may have already fallen off the wagon, become petrified of the next call/email/text/Facebook status and how you might react, or you've become paralysed by the reality of telling this person to take a run and jump, and have gone in search of some information to bolster your decision. And let's be real: you're not dealing with a run of the mill breakup possibly because you weren't dealing with a run of the mill relationship *either*. I don't mean that you weren't dealing with a 'boring' relationship; I mean that if you were in a relationship that had mutual love, care, trust and respect in it even if in the end it ultimately didn't work out, it's unlikely that you'd be applying NC unless one of you had dramatically changed post-breakup.

You're not alone.

Many people including myself, have been in the incredibly difficult position of having feelings for someone and wanting a different outcome so badly but try to essentially 'solve' the problems with the same thinking and behaviours that got us into the relationship in the first place. That's clearly not going to work.

What you must understand at the outset of this process is that **your relationship or 'involvement' is a series**

of events and interactions that, combined together, have formed the **pattern** of your relationship. You are operating off your own series and sequences of **habits** and they are too. Each of your respective habits within this dynamic has taught you both what to expect from each other.

As I've explained to many a person struggling to extricate themselves out of their barely-there relationship, *especially* the ones wondering why they haven't got in touch, or whether *they* should make the first move, the pattern of your relationship and the dynamic that has existed between you helps this person to form assumptions about what you will or won't do. This is *critical* for you to understand.

> **Whatever you have or haven't done previously, they'll make assumptions based on this, and they won't adjust their mindset until they've received significant information via the cues from NC that indicate that the old rules no longer apply.**

This means that even when they're not around, they take enough comfort in the pattern that they feel confident enough to believe that you will, in time, behave in the way that they've come to expect. For some of you, this will mean that they may feel so assured of your adoration, they'll believe that they can get on with their own lives for a long period of time, and then suddenly pop back into your life to disrupt it. They believe that you're so crazy about them that they can feed off this adoration and your distress in your absence.

This is why whatever is the previous **longest** period of time you've been apart or not communicated, you need to exceed this and *then* some. This means that if you've been cut off from each other for a few weeks here and

3-6 months here and there, you need to cut contact for at least 7-12 months to obliterate the pattern. There is no way around this - trust me, many have tried and failed to do otherwise.

Why does this happen? Because even if you think that you've made lots of progress in a few weeks or months but you've never been broken up for longer than a year, the moment you give them the time of day, it does not matter what you say or do, responding is the *only* 'feedback' that they pay attention to. If you've been dealing with someone who blows hot and cold on you, it's only when they realise that you're not doing what they expect, that they get a signal to their brain full of tumbleweed telling them that they need to shift gears and 'strike'. That 'message' indicates that they are not as in control as they think and that you may not be an option anymore which may prompt them to seek confirmation. It's at this point that should they choose to make contact, you have a window of opportunity to show that you mean business and reinforce your boundaries by remaining silent and/or disinterested, by not telling them all about themselves, by resisting the urge to explain that you're ignoring them (no shit Sherlock!), and by not showing up ready for a relationship that they're still not offering.

If you eagerly bathe in the spurt of attention and promises from them, you demonstrate (again) that you're crying wolf – they will perceive your attempts at NC as a 'game' no matter what your original intentions and convictions were and they will feel confident and in control again and they'll either fade out or disappear.

In order for your life to change in a positive manner and to ultimately break free of what may have come to be a very unhealthy dynamic, you need to address your habits. The path that people tend to take is trying to address their behaviour and thinking in order to make themselves more compatible and 'comfortable' with shady behaviour or to 'tweak' the habits in an effort to provoke the desired response from the other party (game playing) and this doesn't work. It just feeds unhealthy habits and ultimately digs you deeper into the unhealthy relationship hole *plus* you become very distanced from your core self – your values, needs, expectations, wishes and ultimately your identity.

When your ex (or soon to be ex) stops taking you seriously and figures out the 'pattern' which is similar to knowing how to jig your lock or break the door code so that they can get back into your life, you will find that NC is the *only* way of communicating that you are not that person anymore, that you're serious, and that the relationship is *over*. If you've been chasing this person around like a blue-arsed fly and they've actually enjoyed the ego stroke to a degree even if things didn't go anywhere, you need to send an entirely different message. Not because you want them to throw themselves at you and beg you to be with them, but because they will have gotten the impression that you're 'there' to be at best taken advantage of and at worst abused *plus* you cannot continue to present yourself as somebody who is OK with not having the basics of love, care, trust and respect.

No Contact is about changing, replacing and even moderating your responses to reduce or neutralise the effect of the cues and triggers, which in turn changes your habits, which in turn changes the dynamic that has existed between you, which in turn changes the pattern. What you do during NC sets clear boundaries for each of you that if you respect these, it not only communicates that you're not going to engage but it also communicates that you're a worthwhile, valuable person who is following through on their personal commitment to being responsible for their happiness.

How An Unhealthy Pattern Is Established

Where there is an unhealthy dynamic, the person knows that when they do X, that you tend to do Y.

X in your relationship is interpreted as either a **cue** (a signal that you respond to in a particular way) or a **trigger** (an event or thing that causes something to happen while also prompting you to respond).

The **action, thought, and emotional responses** that you have to those cues and triggers are **Y**.

X, for instance, could be this person starting to blow lukewarm or even cold and then Y might be you upping the amount of effort you make in an attempt to prompt them into blowing hotter.

Unfortunately, they pick up the cue that when they behave in this manner, you try harder (or do certain things). So they figure out how to get more out of you without having to step up. Or they figure out what they need to do in order to elicit the most personally beneficial response, likely one that doesn't tax them in the areas where they don't want to 'spend'. For example, emotions, effort, time, accountability, responsibility, commitment, money, respect etc.

If you're doing something where on some level they recognise that they're not really matching your efforts or even that they 'obtained' the benefit without the integrity to be genuinely committed to whatever it was that they implied or promised in order to get it, it communicates that not only do they not have to try but also that you're malleable and eager to please.

They deduce that X + Y equals Z and until you stop having the same responses to the cues and triggers in the relationship, this person will continue to believe that it's business as usual. In the meantime you will keep falling into the same traps and wondering why they do what they do.

In the meantime, you've also worked out that when you respond in certain ways that it generates a short-term response that feels like a 'benefit' and this is why you end up crying 'wolf'. The person who keeps threatening to end it does so because it's generated enough of a response to generate a short-term fix but they're also still hoping that 'this time' this person will behave differently… even though they themselves aren't, otherwise they'd make good on what they were saying. Not looking beyond the short-term gratification or even your ego can cause you to attempt to solve or soothe issues with the wrong unhealthy 'fixes' while leaving you exposed to the medium to long-term effects.

NC means that even though the cues and triggers may remain the same, their effect on you is neutralised because you have changed your habits and the thinking attached to them. A lot of the time when I hear from people who are contemplating NC, it's because they've fallen for the *same* con *numerous* times and so each time the object of their affections calls, or says that they've changed, or that they're going to change, or that they're lonely, or that they need them and yada yada yada, they respond and

151

repeatedly end up disappointed and hurt.

If you don't want to continue feeling disappointed, hurt and available for an unavailable, *unhealthy* relationship, go NC and *stick* to NC until you're so far into your new habits that it no longer *matters* what the other party wants or is doing. You'll be enjoying a healthier you so it's not attractive to slide back to habits that you know *don't work for you*.

We teach people what to expect from us and they get an idea of how they think that they can treat us, and if there's little or no real consequences, their behaviour is established as the *norm*. This is why NC is about inserting boundaries into this dynamic. Because if you've been slacking off on the boundaries and even suppressing your own needs, wishes and expectations in the name of 'love', this person will expect that you will do certain things even when then the relationship is over. They'll assume that you're still an option and that you're so mad about them that they can pop up whenever they feel like it. Don't allow this to be true.

An Example of How NC Can Break a Cycle

Here is an example of where a person can get the idea that in or out of the relationship, you are under their thumb and likely to 'respond' in the manner to which they've come to expect, which means that they can extract whatever benefit they've come to enjoy, even if it's as simple as getting an ego stroke from the comfort of knowing that you're still 'there'.

PHASE 1: They Fast Forward you in the early stages of the relationship **PLUS** you respond positively even though the intensity in itself along with the fact that you're strangers should be an 'amber alert' to slow the pace **EQUALS** you both having an intense liaison and they get the impression that you're vulnerable in certain areas and willing to offload your own life and boundaries to buy into fantasy with them.

PHASE 2: They start to ease off and even unfold their true selves which may not be anything like the original 'advertisement' **PLUS** you feel unseated, blame yourself for why they've 'changed' and chase them harder **EQUALS** the balance tips, you've confirmed your vulnerability and in spite of behaving in a less than honourable manner, they're getting more from you instead of you stepping back.

PHASE 3: They end things but then attempt to tap you up for a shag, an ego stroke, shoulder to lean on or whatever **PLUS** you don't tell them to take a run and jump and are willing, albeit not happy about it, to take the crumbs **EQUALS** they know that not only are you willing to accept less than you deserve but they're also being pumped up by your lack of boundaries and are getting the impression that they're *that* special.

PHASE 4: They reduce the contact to a trickle and are no longer able to be reached by phone, are slow to respond to texts or they just get in touch when they feel like it **PLUS** you are trying to reach them, are trying to convince them to treat you better and are even waiting around while they try out others **EQUALS** they learn that you have no limits and that you value their crumbs which suggests that you don't value yourself. They give themselves permission to continue their behaviour in a "Well if they don't value themselves why should I?" attitude as if that's a legitimate reason for their actions when in fact it's their own character and habit regardless of whether you're there.

PHASE 5: Several months or even years go by and they send a text or a message on Facebook **PLUS** you pick up pretty much where you left off with very little barriers to entry **EQUALS** confirmation that you haven't changed and that you're still their backup plan and this in itself may be enough of an ego stroke for them to disappear again.

There is something to be learned from this example – when you're in an unhealthy dynamic with somebody, no matter what they do, you keep attaching the same or similar meanings to their actions and *responding* in a similar manner. If you changed *your* responses while also addressing the *meaning* that you attach to their responses, you would see their lacklustre, neglectful, shady behaviour for what it is. You would also see that regardless of what you perceived this person to be doing in PHASE 1, they *unfolded* into somebody whose actions render them a no-go for a relationship. What happened in PHASE 2 and beyond sheds light on what they were *really* doing in PHASE 1 – using speed and intensity to disarm. When you keep responding to this situation and behaviour by making it about *your* worth, the lack of active response to *their* shady behaviour is giving them airtime and space in your life when you should be recognising what they're doing and telling them to *bounce*.

Now let's imagine that when you experience their behaviour in PHASE 2, you begin NC.

They attempt to reach out to you **PLUS** they're met with radio silence or just a lack of action from you **EQUALS** they receive a cue that something is 'off' and that you haven't responded as they expected.

It's at this point where due to you not responding the way they have come to expect, a sense of feeling out of control is triggered that they likely equate with desire or at the very least curiosity to see if the message they're picking up is true. This is taken as their cue to Up The Ante with the Future Faking and Fast Forwarding including promising to change or claiming that they have, or fixing you with their puppy dog eyes and maintaining how full of regret they are.

They attempt to reach out to you again but with seriously increased effort **PLUS** you still don't respond or say, "I've moved on and I suggest that you move on too" because you've made up your mind that they had their shot and used it to bust boundaries and you're not seeking the fairy tale **EQUALS** they receive a cue that you're not playing ball and may even convince themselves that you're the one that got away.

They keep trying to reach out to you **PLUS** you continue not responding **EQUALS** message loud and clear that their behaviour isn't acceptable and that they may have gotten away with doing certain things but it won't be happening again. In the meantime, you're getting on with your own life and feeling the benefit of not opting back into unhealthiness because you're not hanging your existence on trying to get someone else to change.

But let's imagine that after they were met with radio silence that they upped the ante and due to you being hopeful that they'd changed, you responded and essentially fell off the wagon.

They attempt to reach out to you again but with
seriously increased effort **PLUS** you respond positively
by accepting their contact and taking them at their
word that they've changed **EQUALS** they receive a cue
that you're still interested in what was originally on
offer (but isn't actually available) *plus* they also
receive the cue that as long as they blow hot, you will
respond, maybe not today, maybe not tomorrow, but soon.

Once they're secure in your affections or that they're 'back in control', they gradually or very quickly revert to their previous position. I've heard from thousands of people who been through this, only for the person to literally vanish or do an "I've made a big mistake" within days or hours. That's not something that you need to be laying yourself open to and ultimately your happiness and future shouldn't be resting on the premise and possibility of another person making changes.

You're not going to teach someone to expect different things from you while you're still *in* the relationship with them or when you're trying to get them to change or understand you *after* the relationship – they'll just think that you're venting and that if given a certain amount of time, you'll forget about it or resign yourself to the inevitable. They'll tell you what you want to hear, make a few motions and then passive aggressively or even aggressively edge their way back to their own agenda.

With NC, you can be assured that this isn't going to happen and that ultimately, regardless of whether they're passive aggressive and/or aggressive, you're going to assert yourself in your own life and not be a passenger to their needs, wants and expectations while compromising your own. You *matter* and NC will allow you to realise this and rebuild your life *with* healthier habits.

CAREFUL OF THE BAIT & SWITCH

Picture this: You break up and you do your best to move on but your ex keeps calling and texting and maybe even showing up on your doorstep or at work or pestering friends and family about how they just need you to give them a chance. Sometimes you respond, sometimes you don't. *Interestingly*, sometimes you're met with silence after they've badgered the hell out of you, leaving you wondering if something is wrong or even following it up with increased contact to get clarification.

You might believe that they're pursuing you but actually, *they* may believe that it's you pursuing them.

This means that you can be minding your own business and then end up responding to him/her out of sheer frustration, sympathy, guilt or your struggles with missing them. Because this in their mind confirms that you're still interested (because you're willing to engage), they feel back in control and so they gradually or even immediately become less available while you end up looking like you're the one who is doing all of the pursuing.

This is a classic bait and switch.

It's this sense of the tables being turned that can really mess with your head. You chase, they initially appear to reciprocate, they run. You chase, they back away. You're baited back to this dysfunctional dynamic on the premise of this person being the one near desperate for your attention and validation only to find yourself in that situation.

You back away, they chase, you then reciprocate, they back away. They chase, you ignore, they chase some more, you still ignore them, they chase some more, you start to believe that they must be really serious, you gradually start to respond but you have your guard up, they lay it on thick with a trowel, you gradually let your guard down, they seem to be right there with you, you relax some more, they back away. Can you see what's happening here? No matter who does the chasing, the responding, the ignoring and whatever else, the net result if you respond is that maybe not today, maybe not tomorrow but soon (or maybe it is today or tomorrow!), things will go back to a bad situation *and* you can end up feeling or being treated as if you've been the driver of it all.

The bait and switch is probably one of the most frustrating things that can happen to you with a breakup, especially if you were beginning to feel like you were making strides with your sense of self and especially so if there was a part of you that liked being the one in the driving seat, even if it's an NC one. Due to what happens in the bait and switch, you can be inclined to believe that your efforts have been wasted or that they have all of the 'power' now, but really, they don't have anywhere near as much power as you think. If you heed the message from what they're doing and stick with NC, you won't fall for this situation again *plus* your priority will be ascending into your personal power, not vying for control of the 'relationship empire' with your ex.

NC is absolutely critical because there is no response whether it's to chasing or backing away.

When there are 'power issues', it's never a good thing for a relationship or your sense of self. You can be assured that if you're concerned about power, whether it's getting it back, why they have so much or concerns about the 'upper hand', this is a code red alert that something is seriously wrong. The only power you need to be concerned with is the power to meet your own needs, wishes and expectations while acting in your own best interests. Boundaries will give you the emotional backbone you need.

They can pursue but they're going to be met with the proverbial closed door. It's easy to fall into the trap of believing that they've changed because they're pursuing you so heavily and seem so 'genuine' but if you ride this NC wave for long enough, you'll see that nothing has really changed *plus* if you look at what is happening in the context of your overall relationship, you are likely to recognise a pattern to their (and your) behaviour including the relationship seeming to be at its most desirable to him/her when they're in danger of losing it or they're not sure of your feelings for them.

Self-Preservation Is Invaluable

Distance gives objectivity and perspective and the truth is that when you're right in the thick of things, you're up too close to see clearly. Too much of what's going on gets tied to your worth or how best to avoid 'unpleasant' things like your feelings, conflict, criticism, disappointment and abandonment.

Things are only going to get better if you get out and by making an exit and establishing boundaries, you are protecting yourself from engaging in what can be embarrassing and self-depleting behaviour at best, and at worst, downright humiliating. I've found that when people who are recovering from an unhealthy relationship are struggling, it's not so much with letting the relationship and the person go, but coming to terms with things that they've said and done. Next thing they're wallowing in blame and shame and this can be very destructive to their mental health.

You've gotta know when to fold.

NC teaches you about limits – that's imposing limits about what you're prepared to put up with and saying 'Enough!', and imposing limits on the other party. You'll re-establish your 'powerbase' and start creating a life with meaning... without them. That might be a tough thought to contemplate but a relationship without limits and your personal power is a massacre.

A key thing to recognise is that NC isn't just about not communicating via the phone, email, Facebook etc – it's actually about distancing yourself mentally so that you don't make this person the focal point of your thoughts and activities, because when they are your focus, you're inadvertently communicating with them and continuing to invest emotionally. You're still prioritising this person.

You must communicate with your actions because communication is not all verbal and the object of your NC particularly takes their cues from your actions, or lack of them. If you cut contact but stay mentally connected to thinking about them and the relationship and obsessing over what coulda, shoulda, woulda been, you'll find it all too easy to fall off the wagon. It's extremely difficult to move on if you've brought your life to a complete standstill – you have to get on with things and push through the pain, or your perceived fear of the pain, to find freedom on the other side.

You need to give yourself time and energy.

Going NC made me recognise how much I had neglected myself and when a relationship takes you down this path, whether it's at their instruction or your own unhealthy habits, the very act of cutting contact actually serves as a reminder that you actually *have* a 'self' to preserve in the first place. You will find that how you treat yourself during this process is critical to the success of not only cutting contact and moving on, but also to building your self-esteem.

UNDERSTANDING LOSS

IT'S A LOSS

Irrespective of the length and breadth of your relationship or even if it didn't quite make it to turning into a relationship, you have experienced a loss. Many people who struggle with getting over somebody, haven't fully acknowledged that they *have* experienced loss or they do, but then don't know how to cope with it.

When your hopes and expectations aren't met, this is disappointment. You had hopes for this relationship, for this person and most of all for you.

When a relationship ends or the prospect for one doesn't come to fruition, you have to acknowledge what you hoped and expected for the relationship, this person and even how you saw yourself in the context of these hopes. I think that the latter in particular, especially when you have low self-esteem, is what many people who reel from loss struggle with, because what they'd forecasted for themselves (which may have been an escape from a self that they didn't like) hasn't come to pass. Relationships and another people liking and loving us can represent our last hope when we've pretty much given up on ourselves. When we're of a certain age, it can feel like the stakes are a bit higher so some of our hopes and expectations for ourselves can seem less likely once a relationship ends, which can make it all the harder to come to terms with.

This means that yes you're grieving the loss of this person from your life, but you know what? I've heard so many stories about unhealthy relationships to know that when we truly struggle with letting one go, it's

162

very rarely about the person and it's certainly not about the *real* person. It's more likely that you're struggling with getting over your version of that person (who you hoped they'd become or who you thought that they were) or for the future that you'd hoped for. Or it can be that you have to grieve for the future that you didn't get to have and all of the things that you thought that this person and the relationship meant about you and your life.

Going through NC is about acknowledging, coming to terms with and accepting the loss.

You might want this loss to go away or to pretend that it hasn't happened but this won't serve you and will actually open you up to even more pain and ultimately delay the inevitable. There's no getting away from it. I've spoken to people who have lost loved ones to a bereavement and due to refusal to deal with the loss, they've thrown themselves into another person or engaged in destructive behaviour like drinking too much and doing drugs. As time goes by, though these activities might have served as a distraction, they find themselves facing much bigger problems dealing with a myriad of what can be seen as almost 'dirty' feelings and thoughts caused by the avoidance. On top of this, they *still* have the loss to deal with. When they face this instead of avoiding it, yes it hurts but it's not anywhere near as awful as using a person, alcohol, drugs or whatever to avoid their feelings and to self-harm.

It's better to feel your feelings and process this loss than to avoid it and clog up your feelings with the effect of the destruction.

If you struggle to deal with loss, it's likely to be because you haven't dealt with loss before. This doesn't mean that you haven't *experienced* loss; it means that you've tended to bury your feelings and throw yourself into distractions as your means of recovering. While this can be soothing initially, distraction becomes *destruction* when it impacts on your sense of self. If you're no longer feeling your feelings you're not emotionally available, plus *how* you go about self-soothing has a great deal to do with your recovery. Some people talk a lot, cry, take a lot of baths, walk, do lots of activities, go to support groups etc, whereas some people throw themselves into the next relationship or make, for example, substances the solution to their internal problems. They bounce around from person to person, relationship to relationship or crutch to crutch, or they just keep moving, changing jobs and basically doing whatever they can to distract, and then one day, they realise that they can't run anymore and it's likely to be when they just can't get over somebody or they just can't break an unhealthy tie.

Sometimes the struggle with loss is actually about being used to having everything go your own way so that when it doesn't, you take it exceptionally hard because you haven't learned to deal with disappointment and it takes on a disproportionate magnitude. It feels big because of the way that your ego has taken it, not necessarily because you truly felt deeply. This is why I hear from so many people who struggle to get over someone who, when it comes right down to it, they don't like or are actually completely incompatible with. It's "I can't believe that *they* don't want *me.*"

Loss is what you experience when you feel that you've been deprived of someone or something of value.

Recognising what you feel you've been deprived of or what you consider to be of value will go a long way to helping you come to terms with this loss and to make sense of where you may be stuck.

- Have you been deprived of this person in their truest sense or is it that you feel that you've been deprived of the fantasy version? If it's the latter, you're valuing illusions over reality and this sets you up for extended pain because you're tricking yourself while beating yourself up about something that you know not to be true.

- Is it that you feel deprived because you received a NO, so it feels like you want it and it's so much more valuable now that you know that you can't have it? This is a good time for you to evaluate what you associate 'no' with because if you associate it with being denied something that you want or what people hear when they don't 'deserve' yes, not only will you be particularly rejection sensitive, but you will also have a problem with having, sticking to and even respecting others' boundaries.

- Is it that you believed that you *were* going to 'have' this person or that they were going to leave and they didn't and now you feel robbed or cheated? This is about coming to your expectations and disappointment. You will have to determine whether your expectations were realistic based on this persons actions and words as well as the situation but it's also good to evaluate whether you were disappointed due to something that was out of your control, or whether you think that your disappointment was caused by you? If it's the latter, you are likely blaming yourself for Other Peoples' Behaviour. Instead of experiencing disappointment and recognising the truth of why it happened, you're blaming yourself for whatever they've done as if you provoked the disappointment.

- Is it that you feel like you've compromised yourself so greatly in your quest for love that you almost feel entitled to be with this person as they 'owe' you for the sacrifice? It's tough, but you're not owed a relationship or change from somebody because you were willing to suppress your needs, desires, expectations and basically yourself. That's not a gamble or investment that will ever pay off. It's like expecting to be rewarded for being willing to disrespect yourself, but that's not how you show somebody that you love them.

- Are you overvaluing this person? Do you have them on a

pedestal? Are you almost worshipping a false idol and believing that they had something that would have made you feel worthwhile? What is it they have that you wanted? Understanding what you've overvalued can be a reality check but it can also show you where you need to cultivate the things that you want from others in your own life.

- Is it about you feeling broken by this involvement? Is it that you felt like you had value in this relationship and now you deem you have less due to it being over? This is about the loss of the hope that you had for yourself inside this relationship. The thing is, you don't need this relationship to have hope so how can you put yourself and your life back together and feel valuable on your own two feet whether you're in a relationship or not?

YOU WILL RECOVER FROM THIS

Every day, people experience unimaginable loss in the form of losing a loved one to bereavement. There's a lot that we can learn from this because there are people who are in loving relationships for a number of years and lose their partner suddenly or to a painful illness. Many of these people get back up over time and many live to love and smile again. If people can find meaning in themselves and in their lives after losing a loved one after a relationship spanning fifty years, we *can* recover from involvements that span anything from days to years and we *can* live to love again.

It doesn't mean that these people forget who they loved and it doesn't invalidate the memories. They learn to live with their loss so that they can occupy their lives and even honour the memories of those that they loved who likely wouldn't expect their loved ones to bring their lives to a standstill because they've passed on.

Loss of a loved one whether it's through a breakup or bereavement is scary. It makes us feel insecure and distrusting. We become afraid of allowing ourselves to be vulnerable for fear that if we were to lose someone else from our lives, it would hurt too much. Then we protect ourselves from this by only being involved with people who allow us to remain emotionally safe by letting us love and admire from a distance. And then we end up experiencing even more hurt.

We sometimes judge a current loss on a previous loss even though they may not actually be comparable. While a loss, whether it was someone you dated briefly, experienced unrequited love over, or who you spent many years with, is a loss, the individual loss experiences are different. If, like rejection, we fall into the trap of regarding and treating all losses the same, we trick ourselves into thinking and feeling based on false evidence. We may also do things that we later come to regard as being unproductive and possibly entirely unrelated because we were reacting based on a prior loss instead of the current situation.

It's very possible that this loss may hurt a lot due to previously unprocessed losses so by trying to feel the feelings of *this* loss it's as if you're opening up a dam to feeling the other losses. So you keep trying to avoid the feelings. It's why you may feel like you're madly in love and in so much pain over *this* person, not realising that actually, it's not that; it's that you're experiencing the sum total of all avoided losses.

This loss might feel very big because it's resurrecting other unprocessed losses – a wound is being reopened.

The grief I experienced with the guy at work felt horrific because it was grief over each of my parents, a number of exes and a number of childhood wounds. It explained why he felt so damn critical to my existence. My involvement with him activated something in me and for a period of time, it's like I went to another planet in the pursuit of some fantasy with him that was going to right the wrongs of the past. When things weren't going my way, I came back to earth with a bang and the pain of those realisations and feelings was awful. I felt so unwanted, so unloved, so discarded and like anything of value had been lost because this guy wouldn't leave his girlfriend and pick me.

Loss is very much governed by how you feel about yourself and your life.

People experience a myriad of emotions while going through the grief stages of denial, anger, bargaining, depression and acceptance. Whether they have good self-esteem or not, these stages will happen, it's just that grief takes on a very different form when you really don't like yourself and your life. You may not get to the acceptance stage, or end up accepting the wrong things (false and negative beliefs that can have far-reaching consequences) if, due to being unrealistic about the other party and blaming yourself for what happened, you then internalise these judgments. This will fuel your mentality and actions particularly with regard to how you treat and regard yourself in the future as well as what type of relationships you get involved with.

Right now it might seem unimaginable that you would love someone again or that you would even attempt to date, or just that you will be happy in the future, but you can't know what you're going to feel or experience unless you're planning to remain exactly the same in thought and action as you are right now. You cannot know that this is your *only* relationship or your *only* love or that the amount of happiness you experienced in the past is as good as it gets because you haven't lived all of your life yet (unless you take your dying breath at the end of this sentence) and there isn't a cap on how much happiness you can experience, unless you put that cap there yourself.

I truly felt like I would *never* get over my ex but the truth is, I've felt like I was dying inside over a few relationships yet I lived to tell the tale. The loss we feel is very real but the truth is, sometimes we exaggerate it and defraud ourselves of our present and future by making out like we've been robbed of a fairy tale even if we've really been involved in a Nightmare On Elm Street.

The work you do during NC and grieving your loss is about changing the meaning of these experiences, thoughts and feelings.

By acknowledging and *re*-acknowledging over time what has happened, how you feel, who they are etc, you will face and feel your feelings, go through the emotions and stages of grief and gradually get to acceptance. The more you try to pretend that it isn't a loss or attempt to change a past that's already *passed*, the more you will feel the loss and the more it will appear to grow.

IT'S NOT A WASTE - CHANGE THE MEANING, CHANGE THE FEELING

Acknowledging and gradually accepting that it's a loss doesn't mean that it's a *waste* – not all of our relationships are meant to last, not every person can be the one, and while it isn't often clear at the time when we're hurting, the end is the beginning of something else and likely a blessing in disguise that much further down the line will become clearer to you if you do the grief work now.

It's not a waste. Whatever your relationship is supposed to have been, it's been, even if you would rather that it was something very different.

You've tried and that is not a waste. Most people don't get their relationships right first time. Yes it *is* a pain that after a number of relationships that you may still be experiencing struggles but the number of further struggles and your next relationship can be greatly helped if you use this experience to process not only this loss but all of your losses and *learn* from these experiences. The lesson isn't that you're 'not good enough' or a 'fuck-up'; the lesson is in learning what you can do to better support yourself and what you truly need, want and expect from your relationships. If you've experienced the same thing several times, it's not your worth; it's that you need to change your perspective and choices.

This loss does not have to mean the things that you're thinking that it does so it's critical to evaluate what this loss means to you.

I'm struggling with this loss because it means _____ about my future.

I'm struggling with this loss because it means that I'm _____.

I'm struggling with this loss because it means that I've got to _____.

I'm struggling with this loss because it means that I'm not going to _____.

I'm struggling with this loss because it reminds me of _____ and I interpret this to mean _____ about love/relationships/me.

I'm struggling with this loss because I thought that it would mean that I could _____ .

I'm struggling with this loss because it means that this person was _____.

Whatever it is that you're struggling with, be honest about it and evaluate whether this is true or whether this is based on a generalisation originating from unhealthy beliefs and expectations.

- Is it true that you have no future? How do you know? This can only be true if you decided it and just as you've decided it, you can *un-decide* it too.

- Is it true that this person/relationship was your last chance saloon?

- Is it true that you have little or no options? Break it down and evaluate why you don't have options but more importantly, how you can create options? There's your perception of no options (the path of least resistance) or there's options (the path of change).

- Is it true that because you've experienced this that you've got to lower your standards? Why? What has changed about you? Why do you perceive yourself as not being worthy of dating someone with your standards in tow? I get so many people telling me that because they're in their forties and have experienced a breakup that 'beggars can't be choosers'. Who's the beggar? Why is the forties or any age group beyond that synonymous with being screwed and doomed?

- Is it true that you're not going to be able to do something? If it is, what's your plan B? If it isn't and this can potentially happen now while you're single or in a relationship with somebody else, why are you writing yourself off? How can you go about aligning your actions, thinking and choices towards your needs, expectations and desires?

- Is it true that you've wasted 'everything' or your 'good years'? Look at what you were doing while you were supposedly wasting these years and look at what you can do differently now, because if you sit around thinking that you've wasted it 'all', you will accumulate more regret when you could be focusing on making changes to feel happier now. When you see things in terms of 'waste', you tend to end up going back to or staying in an unhealthy relationship because you want to make it less of a waste by attempting to recoup the investment. Then another few months or even years go by and you kick yourself for not accepting it and moving on, or you resign yourself to remaining forever because you can't see past the regret.

The difficulty with ending what may have come to be a very painful involvement or with trying to let go of your feelings is that you don't know what to do or how to feel. When you lose someone you love to a bereavement and it's been a healthy relationship, you grieve over the happy memories and even some of the tougher times, you feel mad about being robbed of this person and for whatever they've gone through and for the future that they didn't get to have. When you grieve a relationship that never got off the ground or was unhealthy, you're up against a myriad of emotions. You're not sure how to feel and as you start to try to recall the good times they may completely cloud out the not-so-good times for a while, which may actually cause you to feel an even greater loss because your mind ends up being tricked into thinking that this person was exactly how you're portraying them in grief.

Being truthful about your experiences, how you've felt, what you and they have been and done can, when you tot it up, seem so big that to now have no relationship and to need to cut contact can seem like an enormous waste. It can mean so many things whether it's about them or what you've got to sort out in your own life that you may attribute all sorts of negative meanings, which in turn may make you feel like avoiding the loss and going back to make it all mean something else entirely.

You want everything you've felt, been and done to mean something but it's going to mean something entirely different if you continue to engage with this person and end up hurting further.

Yes it's a loss but it's not a waste. It isn't. Some people don't even try; you tried. This isn't about 'mistakes' because it's not a waste if you learn from what was good and bad about your involvement, which can only pave the way to success. We don't get to learn without cutting our teeth on the trial and error of life and its experiences. A mistake really only takes on greater meaning if you won't acknowledge it and that's when you may start to experience regret and feel like you've wasted your life because you persisted with a course of action. But you're trying to do something *now* and if you see this through and grow out of this experience, what has happened could end up being the best thing that ever happened to you because it paves the way to you ascending into being your best you and living a better life.

Change the meaning of this loss and in fact all of your losses and you change the feeling and also change your mentality and actions, which means that you change your present and future. Loss becomes gain. Life is ever changing, ever evolving and renewing. I've seen people triumph out of adversity and loss to dramatically change their lives and experience happiness in a new direction. This can and could be you.

WHAT TO EXPECT WHEN YOU'RE NC

BUCKLE IN

The angst you're experiencing is not unusual – you've experienced a loss, so you have to grieve. That means to experience the myriad of emotions that coming to terms with that loss will cause so that you can heal and move on. You can go up, down, round, sideways about it but the only way to grieve is to go through it. You have to experience the feelings, you have to face your thoughts, you have to face the changes brought about by breaking up, and you have to face yourself. You've also got to reconcile any illusions with reality and ultimately you've got to let go and accept that what you thought would happen isn't going to, so live your life.

When you avoid, you will invite more pain and stunt your growth because you won't be learning from the insights that you stand to gain.

The next few chapters are about letting you know what to expect when you're expecting pain from a breakup, doing NC and also trying to come to terms with what's happened to move forward. I remember opening up *What To Expect When You're Expecting*, the pregnancy bible by Arlene Eisenberg, Heidi E. Murkoff and Sandee E. Hathaway, and while it had a hell of a lot of detail that went right over my head, the overview of each month and stage and typical questions at that time was very useful. Think of the following chapters as a rough guide for up to one year of NC.

Note that every person is different so you may stay in a stage longer than someone else or you may sail through it sooner. It's not a competition and ultimately giving you a sense of what to expect is actually there to help you identify and understand what you might be feeling or going through at a particular point in time. I get so many people asking me, "Natalie, is it normal to be feeling vengeful?" or "Is it normal to be doing really well, to realise it and then go into a slump?" and so use this section to internalise that you're entirely normal and *definitely* not alone. One day you're no longer NC – you're just living your life. You end up moving so far ahead that it doesn't matter whether they do or don't make contact or whether they attempt to get back together, because you're strong enough to deal with whatever comes along.

BUT SERIOUSLY, HOW LONG IS THIS GOING TO TAKE?

They say that time heals all wounds and while yes it does take time, it's actually what you do and *think* during that time that affects the healing process. Trust me, if you think that you can break up now and that by default in a year's time this will be a distant memory without you having to put some concerted effort into the initial cutting contact and then the grief work, you will only set yourself up for pain. There's no hard and fast rule and grief in itself isn't linear, so your grieving isn't an identikit version of someone else's. Plus you're going to take steps forwards and then go back a little or even a lot and then make gains again. The biggest influencers of how long it's going to take are as follows:

Your self-esteem. Have an honest conversation with yourself about whether you're neglecting or nurturing yourself. If you have low self-esteem at the start of NC, it's going to take time *especially* if you don't take on board that you're going to have to nurture yourself during this time by treating yourself with love, care, trust and respect while talking and supporting yourself through some of the difficult decisions you make along the way. Remember that it takes more than going through the motions of life to take care of yourself - if your head is polluted with negative thoughts, this directly affects your recovery time.

Your resilience for disappointment and rejection. Take it badly, keep revisiting it, judge yourself harshly, persecute yourself, or do things to counter the sense of rejection and disappointment that only end up causing you even more pain, and this is going to take you longer than it would have done.

Your lifestyle. If you occupy your life as in you reside in it, value it, fill it up with things that meet your needs, expectations and wishes, you will feel happy and that will help your recovery. If your life comes to a standstill, you become a recluse, or you do things that basically detract from yourself like hanging out with a bad crowd, ditching work, sacking off friends and family, it will take longer.

Your experiences during the relationship. If it was particularly traumatic, you may need more time simply because you need to do some healing work to recover from the trauma.

The length of the relationship. There's no hard and fast rule. I've heard from people who after two years, are *still* trying to recover from a relationship that *never* happened and people who it took several months to a year or so to get over a much longer relationship. Note that if it ends up taking you more than year to get over a relationship that didn't start or was only a few months, it means that too much of yourself was invested in what you thought might happen or in this person's perception of you.

Your beliefs. The fact that it may take longer for someone who never even had a relationship to recover tells you that it's how you judge yourself and your options after the breakup that means a great deal. Every single person I've heard from who cannot let go even when the amount of time not letting go significantly outweighs the involvement, is struggling with beliefs and possibly shame.

Previous losses. Tying into the resilience for disappointment and rejection, it may take you longer to get over a breakup if it resurrects a previous loss.

Unforeseen circumstances. Unfortunately even when we're hurting, life goes on and sometimes that means that we can feel kicked when we're down. If you lose your job, or you have a big fall out with a close friend or family member, there's a bereavement, you lose confidence in your appearance, you experience a trauma, or even try to move on and experience a setback, this can affect your recovery time. You will have to put in more effort to take care of yourself and you may need to draw on your support base.

Being avoidant. If your typical response to uncomfortable thoughts, feelings and situations is to do something to limit, distract from, or avoid these, breakups will be tricky for you as you may have delayed reactions to your experiences as you may be so used to what you do that you won't recognise your own avoidant behaviour. If this is you, I would recommend that you check in with your feelings about this breakup each day by keeping a Feelings Diary so that you can build self-awareness.

WHAT YOU'RE LIKELY TO BE EXPERIENCING AT THE OUTSET

WATCH OUT FOR

Trying to avoid your emotions
Willpower supply issues
Reconciliation attempts
Debriefing sessions
Text and Facebook anxiety

Grief, denial, self-blame, misplaced guilt, hate, desperation, struggling with willpower, feeling bereft, obsessing, irrationality, desperate urge to call, desperate to know what they're doing, missing the routine, missing the certainty of the uncertainty, skipping work, feigning sickness, not eating, overeating, hanging around on dating sites looking for attention, temptation to regress or you do regress, looking for excuses to see your ex, driving past their work, trying to get information from their or your friends, over analysis, attention seeking, checking their dating profiles, drama seeking, hanging up calls, most likely time to wind up in bed together, emotions being up and down, anger at one or both of you, frustration, impatience that you're not instantly over it, on a high from feeling empowered, seized by fear, fragility that may catch you off guard, feelings and thoughts coming at you in waves, temptation to switch from this rollercoaster to the old rollercoaster with them, throwing yourself into work, soothing with inappropriate solutions including sex, drugs and alcohol.

KEY GOALS

To do everything possible from your end of things to cut contact and keep at a safe distance.

To begin to recognise your feelings along with the cues, triggers and typical responses.

To face off temptation and difficult situations that may arise but to respond differently and learn from each experience.

Some days you'll win and others you won't but each day you'll learn.

The bedding-in period is where you're going to cut your teeth on making the difficult decisions and having to react in a non-typical fashion to thoughts, feelings, and situations that present themselves. This time is for you to take the steps that you need to cut contact and to acclimatise to the change and teethe your way through the process – you've got to get on board with NC.

This is a good time for you to throw your heart and soul into letting your emotions come up to the surface. If ever there is a time when you have a license to wallow, this period is it so don't be surprised if you stay in bed a bit (or a lot more), cry, beat your pillows, tell the story of the fallout numerous times, and feel sorry for yourself. It's all normal. Try not to hold back because while keeping up a brave face has its uses in public places, trying to pretend that you're not hurt and upset will only make the process harder, especially as you may have an even more painful delayed reaction.

Like any habit that needs to be changed, it's during this period that you're going to need the most willpower as you adopt different responses and restrain yourself. Depending on your situation, you may be having to rebuff their attempts at contact, or it could be that you're restraining yourself from reaching out, or it might be that they're not reaching out and that in itself can hurt a lot.

Expect this phase to last for at least six weeks, especially if there are some habits that you've got to focus on. But depending on what happens during this time and other factors that affect grieving time, this could run into a few months. If this was a short involvement and you've cut contact just to draw a line under it, you may find that it takes as little as a week but again it all depends on how affected you've been by this involvement. If you're still doing a lot of this stuff when you're heading towards four to six months and beyond, it's an indication that you're likely being very reactive and almost putting yourself through your own Groundhog Day by pressing reset despite the pain you feel from seeking short-term results. If you're going through a lot of this stuff and it's running beyond six months or even beyond a year, you've got to stop fighting and kidding yourself that you can do this without some additional support and look at getting some professional help.

WHAT YOU'RE LIKELY TO BE EXPERIENCING ONCE THE INITIAL DUST HAS SETTLED

WATCH OUT FOR

Getting high on drama

Feeling bored due to loss of 'purpose' and 'fidgeting' your way into breaking NC

False confidence

Feeling better but possibly not wanting to

Feeling guilty about your decision

Back to work, back to friends and family, starting to sound like a broken record, feeling very sorry for yourself, thinking your friends don't understand, desire to be feeling as bad as you were in the first month because you acknowledge on some level that you actually feel better, start seeing him/her and the relationship for what it is, anger at yourself, anger at him/her, immense pain, falling off the wagon territory, laying the foundations for rebuilding yourself and your life, scared of how much time has passed, wondering what if things could have been different.

KEY GOALS

To establish the new routine of not being with / reaching out to your ex.

To start learning to solve issues that you would have previously relied on your ex for via your own means.

Try to spend as much time as you can in the present.

You made the right decision – support it. If you're not supporting your decisions, you're not supporting you.

You'll probably find that because you wallowed in your pain prior to this, you'll actually be sick of feeling like this which will prompt you to start getting out and doing different things and integrating yourself back into life. If you haven't been going to work, have been calling in sick, being generally unreliable, and being emotionally and potentially physically absent to friends and family, this is your time to get up off your bum and force yourself back into life, whether you feel like you want to or not.

You're hurting and your brain is likely on overtime, but be assured that you will actually start to feel the benefits of NC if you're getting on with your life. It's when your life comes to a standstill and you won't start creating one with a new meaning that doesn't include your ex, when you may feel that NC is a pain in the ass that you'd rather exchange for the pain of them.

You may go through a false sense of security that convinces you that you're doing so well, it will be no harm to have them in your life as a friend. Don't, it's too soon and it may plunge you into more pain. If you do break NC, you may feel like you're back to square one but you'll find that even though you have some recovery to do, that you get over the fall quicker than you would have done previously. On the flipside, you may be tempted to hold onto them out of a sense of pride initially as you may not want to admit that it's gone wrong, and if this is the case, you may find it more painful than when you first started out. Try not to beat yourself up by calling yourself a failure because this isn't about failing; it's about realising that you hit a bump in the road and that whilst you have progressed, you still have some road to travel on your journey. If you have fallen off the wagon, you need to get back on it as soon as possible.

It's very possible that you might start to convince yourself that you've committed some sort of wrongdoing by going NC or even convincing yourself that maybe whatever happened in the relationship was warranted hence you're now a 'bad person' or at the very least a 'wrong person' for going NC. Guilt is something that lots of people struggle with but it's important to realise that the presence of guilt is not the same as there being a presence of wrongdoing and even though you may have done things that you regret, it doesn't invalidate your decision to do NC.

You may feel anger creeping up on you or it may have hit you full force or maybe you're already feeling quite down. Depending on where you are with grieving the loss, you may find this period of settling in after the initial decision to go NC quite tricky because you're trying to settle in while possibly feeling very angry and/or very down or a rollercoaster of emotions. You won't have that initial high of embarking on NC and you may feel more aware of time and what lies ahead or what you *think* lies ahead. You may wonder if you've made a big mistake or wobble over it being too hard but when you feel like this is when you need to sit through the feelings and push to the other side, not give in.

If you were quite busy during the initial phase, you may be tired of doing the whole going out and being super-busy thing and that's understandable. This may mean that you're struggling with boredom or just realising that you don't know a great deal about yourself or how to 'entertain' yourself. Don't let this get you down and instead see NC as an opportunity to find out what makes you tick.

Grief and NC aren't linear so it's not set in stone about when this phase will kick in but it's likely to be after a month. If it was a very short involvement, you may find that you move into this phase after a week or so, simply because to be in the initial phase for several weeks or months may be disproportionate to the original involvement and in turn, you may feel bored due to the lack of purpose because going NC in these circumstances may have given you a 'buzz'. Be careful of looking for attention elsewhere – learn to just be with you.

WHAT YOU'RE LIKELY TO BE EXPERIENCING ONCE YOU'RE IN A ROUTINE

WATCH OUT FOR

Relaxing a bit too much and convincing yourself that you're ready for contact or 'friendship'
Deciding that they 'must' have changed
Giving yourself a hard time if they're not in touch
Waves of anger and sadness
Missing him/her
Impatience that your feelings won't go away

Likely to realise that you're further along than you thought, tempted to make friends with your ex, may feel brave enough to hang out with mutual friends or just friends of theirs who are nosing about, feelings of anger and sadness possibly coupled with the desire to break no contact just so that you can tell them all about themselves or pour out your feelings, impatience about not being over them or not in a new relationship, tempted to believe he/she misses you, tempted to believe that they've changed, may fall off the wagon simply due to recognising that you're doing well and fearing having to be done with it, worried about whether they've moved on, suddenly realising that you're happy, contemplating dating, may feel necessary to set boundaries with other people in your life now that you have a greater awareness, starting to get back into the swing of things with work and your social life, may be feeling lonely if your lives were quite intertwined or you've been isolating yourself, may suddenly be hit with the grief after an initial few weeks and months of being quite upbeat, growing self-awareness due to the self-knowledge you're gaining from the process, suddenly dreaming about your ex and convincing yourself that it has more meaning than it does, visiting psychics.

KEY GOALS

To extend new habits into months.
To work on processing feelings and thoughts.
To start getting your life back on track.

Having your own back no matter what is invaluable and will give you the strength to act in your best interests, even when you have to make the tough decisions and say NO to yourself.

This is a transitioning period where you're shifting from acclimatising to the process of NC to being a bit more natural with the habits and trying to put the focus positively on yourself as opposed to feeling that your life is being directed by the effects of this previous relationship. It's finding that balance between doing NC but at the same time not wanting to feel like you're a Rottweiler patrolling the perimeter or that you're on edge all the time. You're not over this person but you're not raw either although you may have days where you're caught off guard. Anger and a myriad of emotions that are attached to it are going to come at you in waves – don't avoid your feelings but don't feed them with negativity either.

Habits that you've been working on should be starting to take hold although you will still have to teethe and tweak here and there so it's important to listen to yourself. Because you're moving out of those initial days, weeks and even months, what this stage is really crucial for is learning to deal with things that have typically involved you responding in an unhealthy way and/or reaching out to your ex in a different way. You might be finding having to make these changes or just NC as a whole, a bit daunting or may even feel frustrated that your life hasn't been transformed beyond belief, but stay the course. It hasn't been that long and impatience isn't going to help.

If you fell off the wagon in the early days or had several attempts at NC and then finally saw the light, you may find that you enter into this phase with a great deal of resolve. Due to feeling a bit more consistent and in control, you may feel less prone to being emotionally vulnerable at the drop of a hat and feel more trusting. That said, if you haven't had any dealings with your ex during the bedding in period, you may find that your awareness is heightened about the possibility of them reaching out and feel unsure about how you're going to deal with it. It's important to remember that you have to plan for success instead of worrying yourself into believing that you're going to screw up. While of course you might hear from your ex during the first phase, what tends to happen is that *just* as it seems like you're moving on with your life and that you're over them, they'll pop up in your life. They don't have a homing device but it is a time period (depending on the length of your relationship) that tends to spark some level of curiosity and "I can't believe he/she hasn't spoken to me in three months... hmmm... Let me just confirm that I'm not an asshole..."

If you're feeling quite confident in this phase, be careful of using this buoyancy as a cue that you should start dating or even enter into a new relationship *especially* if it's with a friend who has been consoling you, another ex or even one of this ex's friends. You may be overestimating your capacity and readiness for a relationship and so you have to make sure that you're not avoiding your feelings and thoughts. If for whatever reason this doesn't work out, it's likely to reopen the wound if you didn't *heal* the wound in the first place.

Again, the timeframe on this phase isn't set in stone. It might not last very long or it may last for beyond six months and it again depends on what you were dealing with in the relationship as well as what might be going on during the time of NC. The main thing you need to keep an eye on is working through the anger and allowing your feelings to surface all while nurturing yourself when you may be tempted to do something else.

UNDERSTANDING THE NC GRIEF STAGES: DENIAL

WHAT TO EXPECT

Can't believe this is happening.

Wondering if it's possible to give them another chance.

Wondering what was real and what was fake.

Analysing what was said and done and often blaming yourself for things that they did, which is actually a form of denial that displaces the responsibility.

Temptation to break no contact.

Feeling like you're in a fog.

Trying to be their friend.

Waiting for the I Made A Mistake Call… or text/email/tweet or Facebook message…

Whether the final step into taking the plunge into NC is prompted by anger or just knowing that you can't take another day of dealing with this person, you will experience denial although it may be to greater or lesser degrees depending on your circumstances. You may have been in this stage since before you broke up or initiated NC and it starts with struggling to believe that this is happening to you and that you *really* have to make this decision and do this. When this has been going on for a while, you'll have known that something was wrong but weren't able to admit it, possibly because you hoped that things would get better or because you judged yourself over this realisation and worried about having made a mistake or even held yourself entirely responsible for the situation, including their behaviour.

You might have hoped it was a 'rough patch' even if it has been a rather extended one. If you've broken up before, you might have struggled to admit that this is not the type of relationship where you can stay friends immediately or you may have overestimated your capacity to cope and it's turned out that it's too raw to remain in contact with them. Sometimes it's as simple as being unwilling to admit that you're just not compatible, irrespective of how you each feel.

If you are in denial about how serious the issues are in your relationship, you may flip flop in indecision about NC and be tempted to fall off the wagon.

If you're in denial about the relationship being well and truly over, you may undermine your own NC efforts by quietly or openly seeking validation from them so you don't feel rejected and so that you can keep the relationship alive.

During this stage, you can battle with the realisation that this is over for good or this sense of feeling rejected like, "I can't believe that they don't want me!" If you had some underlying motivations to use NC to jolt them into stepping up and giving you what you want, they're most likely to be flushed out during this time and when they reveal themselves, it may hurt because you will have to face what you've been putting off (that this isn't working or that these 'strategies' are actually hurting you more than helping you). It's also likely to bring up a myriad of difficult emotions including frustration, anger and even shame because you won't want to believe that the truth is the truth.

Denial is a natural and important part of the grieving process. It's your mind's way of doing a bit of a shuffle and allowing yourself to process reality in more palatable, digestible chunks. This stage of the grieving process though, only really 'works' if you're not typically someone who tends to treat truths that don't suit your agenda as unacceptable.

The lower your self-esteem or the bigger an issue you have with dealing with disappointment and perceived 'rejection' or 'abandonment,' the messier this stage can get due to untruths you're feeding yourself about you and this person, including blaming yourself for their actions.

When you've been denying, rationalising, minimising and excusing things that you really needed to be allowing into your consciousness and having an active response to, the breakup and ensuing NC is tough because it's like doing an end of year accounts and having to pull out all of your receipts and unsorted paperwork from under the carpet. Grief is partly about reconciling the perception that you had of things with the reality and there can be some incredibly painful realisations, which is why you may find it easier to try and pursue this relationship against the odds rather than face the truth.

You wonder what was real and what was fake.

It's at this stage of struggling with working our reality that you may respond to the difficult emotions and thoughts by reaching out. Unfortunately this is a bad idea, simply because it's just adding more onto your pile of things to work out, deny or feel bad about. You may feel tempted to break NC because you simply want to prove that your perception of things is or was true. If they respond, you'll feel temporarily validated until it becomes apparent that actually, the same issues still prevail and the relationship you want and hope for cannot happen.

The truth is – and you may find this difficult to digest – that you will struggle with this stage if you don't tend to be realistic about people, simply because you will think X and then do Y and then get upset about Z outcome because of the denial-based logic and reasoning applied to your course of action. You'll kid yourself that they'll come back soon or that you can both be friends or that you can even squeeze in one last shag for old time's sake and then your heart will hurt, as will your mind over the reality that you're neglecting yourself.

This is also a stage where you've got to be careful of secretly holding out hope and waiting around. Even a teeny little bit of hope is enough to create a large vulnerability. I've seen people go through NC but hold onto this hope and it becomes a block to truly being there for themselves never mind for a new relationship.

If you persist in denial, not only does this take you out of reality and so distort everything that you're thinking and doing, but it's highly likely to result in you becoming trapped in your feelings and thoughts, which in turn can lead to you doing stuff off the back of these that you may later struggle to come to terms with.

UNDERSTANDING THE NC GRIEF
STAGES: ANGER

WHAT TO EXPECT

Being very angry with yourself.

Being very angry with them.

Being tempted to lash out and tell them all about themselves.

Feeling consumed by your feelings.

Possibly contemplating revenge.

Ruminating, often at night or when you're at a loose end, which, if you respond to this, may result in you texting or calling them.

Feeling like you can't move on.

Feeling bitter, despondent, or even believing that you're miserable while they're living the life of Riley.

If they've moved on, "Why them and not me?"

Raking over previous hurts and rejections and even feeling angry with your family due to, for example, childhood issues.

After denial tends to come anger, a very natural but unfortunately very often misunderstood emotion that comes about from feeling that you've been wronged, offended, denied or even made a fool of. This stage may have actually started before your relationship ended but you either kept a lid on your true feelings or have been going back and forth with them. It can also be a delayed reaction to certain truths or realisations coming to light and sometimes, you just feel angry because your hopes and expectations for the relationship didn't come to fruition.

Anger is a normal, *valid* emotion that we all have to experience and go through because it helps us to make sense of our feelings and thoughts. By recognising our feelings of anger and allowing ourselves to feel and express them, even if it's to ourselves, we get to understand ourselves further and validate ourselves. Anger is actually a normal emotion and is a natural part of grieving the loss of your relationship. When you have been wronged or have done stuff that has not been in your own best interests, it is *OK* to be angry. It is *normal* to be angry.

Many people have some level of shame or even snobbery attached to anger as if only certain types of people get angry or that it's 'wrong' to feel it or even that all anger equals rage, which isn't true. Rage is violent, uncontrollable anger. The associations you make with anger are likely due to early, or certainly very difficult, experiences of someone else's anger or your own and this can affect your ability to not only express anger when you're pissed off, but to also experience it as part of the grieving process. You may feel guilty for feeling it or even angry and so this period of NC can end up being a good time to not only learn how to sit with your feelings but to address your relationship with anger.

Denial has a lot to do with what you might experience during this stage due to painful realisations that may come off the back of stepping into reality. You will also find that the more people-pleasing and turning red-light behaviour green that you did in the relationship, the more hurt and angry you're likely to feel. Plus if there has been any deception, humiliation or just what is perceived to be rejection, you may feel akin to one of those pressure cookers that's been left on for too long.

- You may find it easier to be angry with yourself rather than your ex, which is how you get into blame and shame territory.
- You might be caught off guard by how angry you are if you've suppressed your needs, expectations and wishes.
- You may feel angry a lot of the time (especially if you keep feeding it with blame, shame or snooping) and find it difficult to move past it. You end up being angry about the fact that you're angry.
- You may be hijacked by your anger and act upon it. In turn this may prompt you to do things that may cause you to feel embarrassed or even humiliated, which in turn will create a vicious cycle of anger and shame.
- You might be angry with a lot of people due to this making you see where you may be being taken advantage of or seeing the cumulative effect of the injustices you've experienced at the hands of others.

THERE ARE KEY REASONS WHY YOU WILL FEEL ANGRY

- ❖ Feeling frustrated and unloved/uncared for and disrespected because you were undervalued. **No Contact teaches you to value yourself.**
- ❖ Feeling frustrated and unloved/uncared for and disrespected because your trust has been abused. **No Contact distances you from the source of your pain and teaches you to trust yourself and have boundaries.**
- ❖ Feeling frustrated and unloved/uncared for and disrespected because you feel shame. **No Contact teaches you not to take on blame and shame for other people's behaviour but to learn**

positively from what has happened instead.

❖ Feeling frustrated and unloved/uncared for and disrespected because you feel rejected. **No Contact, in distancing you from the source of your pain and getting you to focus on yourself and create boundaries, gets you to reject any unacceptable behaviour.**

It's this sense of injustice – you want things to be fairer and may feel like you're not getting your chance to correct that wrong. If you become consumed by this injustice, you may perceive it as being about your worth or become consumed by the desire to make things right. It's during this stage that you may feel particularly tempted to tell your ex all about themselves. You may end up with a whole load of angry draft emails and texts or find yourself halfway to their house ready to confront them only to turn around with tears streaming down your face. You might destroy every photo you have and then be stricken with remorse and regret and so spend a huge chunk of time sticking them back together or printing them out.

You may find this stage all-consuming and it might hang around for a while or you may find that you vacillate between this stage and others. All of this is normal and it either means that you're circling back to resolve elements of your grief that are cropping up or it means that you might need to either ease up on giving yourself a hard time or make a very conscious decision to let something go that you keep revisiting. That's not about ignoring your feelings but if you keep ruminating over the same thing but aren't going beyond this, the anger is becoming a security blanket that's also corroborating a story you keep telling yourself.

There are going to be bad days, really bad days and also OK, good and even brilliant days. Some days you'll win and some days you'll lose but the net result if you stick with NC and nurturing yourself is that you'll make gains.

It's critical to work your way through anger and have some of those bad days... and then come out the other side of it. Each time you do, you learn a little bit more about yourself. Working through means getting it out of your head by talking and writing about it. It's making sense of it, it's crying, it's sometimes having a damn good scream when the music is up loud or when no one is home.

It's important to grasp that feeling anger doesn't mean that you are 'correct' in every perception attached to it or that you're making a permanent judgment about the situation but it *is* about recognising that you are feeling these feelings for a *reason* and that in itself is *valid*. Your feelings are yours. If you allow yourself to be angry, you get to understand the reason, you get to process it and you ultimately get to learn from it and better serve your own needs, wishes and expectations.

Anger when processed allows you to positively adjust your perspective. Left unattended, anger will warp your perspective and eat you up.

If you don't allow yourself to feel all of your emotions during NC and beyond, you won't be able to recognise what you were missing from this relationship so that you can be better equipped to cultivate these elements in your own dealings with yourself and be more aware next time of how to avoid this situation, or to seek out what you truly want and need.

The key now is to work your way through the anger rather than rendering yourself immobile by being trapped in it. Until you let it out, it will rattle around in your head, distorting your perception and perspective, and eating away at your sense of self. That anger isn't just going to disappear – it has to go somewhere and right now it's in you.

UNDERSTANDING THE NC GRIEF STAGES: BARGAINING

WHAT TO EXPECT

Coming up with ideas that would enable you to return to the relationship –
imagining deals and compromises.
Praying that if X happens you'll do Y.
Possibly breaking NC in an attempt to enter into negotiations.
Ruminating over the 'If only's.

Bargaining is something that you will have started experiencing pretty much as soon as it became apparent that the relationship wasn't going to work out and it's where you make deals and come up with compromises, either privately in your head or with the other person.

If the relationship isn't over yet or you haven't started NC, you'll come up with a compromise to prevent the relationship ending and it's probably a compromise that has you compromising yourself. For example, OK maybe I can try an open relationship if it means that I don't lose him/her.

You might bargain with whoever you believe in, with yourself, or even with this person including making promises about what you'll do if your prayers come true.

You might bargain with this person and attempt to negotiate yourself into a better position e.g. I won't make any demands on you so that you stay.

When you've cut contact and experienced the denial and anger, at the times when you feel tempted to break NC, it's because you're bargaining with yourself or even with a higher power that you believe in. If you actually fall off the wagon, you will find yourself bargaining with either yourself or them, or both, and this will likely result in you being compromised because you're not really coming from a place of logic or even dignity – the desire to bargain is being driven primarily by your ego and possibly even desperation.

When you enter into the bargaining stage, you may feel buoyant due to the fantasy playing out in your head even if it's tinged with blame and shame such as "If only I'd been slimmer then they wouldn't have wanted to look elsewhere" or "If only I'd answered the phone that night" or even "If only I hadn't listened to my [concerned] friends and family."

For a time, even if it's only for a very short period of time, you feel wildly hopeful due to what this bargain appears to represent – hope – and unfortunately this sets you up for experiencing the disappointment all over again because you may have temporarily believed that it was all going to work out.

Of course it's very possible that it's at this stage that you might be tempted to break NC and many people find this confusing because they think, "Well I've been through denial and anger so why now?" but sometimes in response to us recognising that we're processing and distancing ourselves emotionally from someone, we sabotage so as not to face the changes or possibly uncomfortable feelings that we're dealing with. We become scared and it seems easier to take a punt on someone else changing than it does to take a punt based on us having to make all of the effort for ourselves.

This is a stage that you may not linger in for too long. After it becomes apparent that you're not able to strike a deal, you may try to buy more time to come up with a new plan (shifting back to denial) or move into a renewed phase of anger or feel depressed due to the loss of hope and the realisation that what you're doing is real – that NC isn't going to prompt this person to spontaneously combust into The Ideal Human™.

The key to turning bargaining into something productive and moving beyond this stage, is to keep your feet in reality with a clear, real image of who the other person is, and make constructive deals with yourself.

When we are tempted to break contact, we're bargaining, but we make decisions in isolation often not based on reality but a remarkable set of circumstances that will need to come about if only the other party changes.

When the bargaining stage really kicks in during your grieving, it's when you're trapped by your feelings and trying to stem the feeling of the perceived rejection and the loss by contemplating seeking attention from the source of your pain (your ex) so that you can feel less rejected and avoid working your way through the loss.

If you allow yourself to be hijacked by the bargaining stage, you'll come up with deals and bargains that will allow you to have the relationship on any terms rather than none at all, which is where you will end up being compromised, especially as you will end up doing things that not only detract from yourself but that open you up to pain, and may also embarrass or even humiliate you.

For example, I'd rather have him on any terms than be without him. Things could work out because I'll be more understanding and when I get back in touch with him, he'll be relieved to have me back, see the error of his ways, and we can make the relationship work.

UNDERSTANDING THE NC GRIEF STAGES: DEPRESSION

WHAT TO EXPECT

Being caught off guard by what feels like overwhelming loss at times.

Crying suddenly.

Feeling despondent.

Feeling rejected – "I wasn't good enough for…"

Previous loss and anger that you haven't resolved returning to the fore – you may feel very sad about other areas of your life that this relationship helped you to avoid.

Blaming yourself.

Realising that it's been X weeks or months since you started NC and feeling bad about having to do it in the first place.

Feeling that you've lost your investment.

Focusing on regrets.

Feeling like you'll never get over this even though you're likely forgetting that you've actually been feeling overall better for being out of the situation.

Feeling guilty even though you really don't need to

Being freaked out about not thinking about them all the time and then going into thinking overload.

Secretly or even openly being afraid of moving on and having to get on with your own life and having a new purpose.

Depression is unexpressed anger turned inwards and also a very deep sense of sadness and disappointment that you don't know where to place, so it's put on you. It happens after you've been through the other stages and have started to realise that the relationship is really is over, that NC really is needed and the other person isn't going to change. That understanding that this is it can leave you feeling very down. Realising that whatever bargains that you make with yourself or with them are a waste of time or at the very least very painful can feel so disheartening because it means accepting that it is over and you may not feel like your heart can cope with that just yet.

You may move through this stage very quickly or it may linger, especially if exiting this relationship is causing you to have to face up to other aspects of your life that you're not happy with.

Even though NC allows you to regain your power and rebuild your life, you may feel depressed that you didn't have enough power to have them come crawling back on their hands and knees in remorse, to make them change their ways, or to even feel enough regret to try to break down your NC walls.

You may feel so much pain at the loss of the relationship or still feel like you're drawn to them even if you're not acting upon it and it may feel depressing because you really wish you didn't feel like this.

This feeling can be especially difficult to deal with if on the face of it you recognise how toxic this person was and yet you still feel drawn to them. You may end up feeling a great deal of blame and shame and what's easily forgotten is that you're human, you loved and you wanted to be loved. Sure you recognise that this person is certain things but you're grieving and it takes some time for the feelings to catch up with the reality. Being impatient with yourself or judging yourself for not being over it faster isn't going to help you.

You've likely been very affected by your involvement if you need to go NC so you have to realise that it's entirely understandable that it's taking time. What you have to be careful of is letting the disappointment eat you up because when the depression stage lingers, it's because you're judging yourself in some way. You may also still feel entitled to the desired outcome that you envisaged regardless of the fact that the outcome didn't match the person or the actual relationship you were in.

Sometimes when you're NC you get depressed because realising it's been a month, or 6 weeks or many more months and that you still think about them frustrates you and you feel angry because you convince yourself that they must still matter. Then you feel guilty that they still matter and get caught in a cycle of feeling that you're letting yourself down. I should add that sometimes the whole thinking about them is actually habit, not any real sign of feeling towards this person!

We can feel odd if we don't think about them all the time, much like people who grieve someone after they die and then feel weirded out that they're moving on.

It's also the loss of hope or even the activation of shame that can be experienced due to an involvement. This person may seem like they walked off with all of your possibilities or even worse, it may seem that they walked off with the knowledge of something that you judge yourself about the harshest. If you allowed yourself to be vulnerable, if you shared something and then it was used against you, even though you've actually got nothing to be ashamed of, it feels like what you shared or did has been used against you. This in itself is enough to scare you off the possibility of trying again so this in itself can leave you feeling depressed about your prospects.

Loss and disappointment is something that most people struggle to come to terms with to some degree and it's made all the more sad by a pervasive culture of not taking mental health seriously and attaching unnecessary stigma to it. It's no wonder that so many people end up keeping their feelings to themselves when really, what they need to do is talk about what's happened instead of locking themselves away in this isolated bubble of blame, shame and rumination.

It is totally OK to have down times whether they last a day, a few days, or even a few weeks. These feelings and thoughts are about you processing the loss on a deeper level and if it didn't hit you at some point you would be missing an important part of grieving (even if overall the relationship didn't last for long). If your relationship was a lengthy one or quite traumatic, it may take months to work through – but you'll get there. If you take care of yourself and work your way through your feelings and at the same time don't get hijacked by them and throw yourself onto the front line of pain with him/her, you will come out the other side. If you beat yourself up, let the thoughts rattle round and round your head, opt out of your day to day life, and don't treat yourself with the love, care, trust and respect that you deserve, it will take longer.

This stage is normal and expected but it is the judgements you make about yourself and trying to hide away from your feelings that can lead to full depression that can greatly affect your life. You may feel very down but you may not actually be experiencing depression in its fullest sense – it's when you continue to feel down over an extended period of time and you can't seem to pull it back, that you can find yourself needing to take action which may include seeing a professional.

UNDERSTANDING THE NC GRIEF STAGES: ACCEPTANCE

WHAT TO EXPECT

One day you realise that you can think about them without your heart sinking to the floor.

You suddenly realise you've been so busy and happy that you haven't thought or even dreamt about them for a while.

You're making and realising plans.

You feel quietly happy about yourself.

There may be a little sadness but nothing that pulls you down – you know that you did the right thing.

If they attempt to contact you, it doesn't feel like the sky is falling in.

You don't think of yourself as NC; you're just living your life.

You'll stop trying to be The Good Girl / Guy doing the right thing for them and instead doing the right thing for you.

You'll stop trying to be friends with them or making plans to be friends with them in the future.

You won't feel angry or sad whether it's towards yourself or them – you'll find yourself increasingly at peace. Period.

You'll stop wishing that things had been or were different.

You'll stop trying to rationalise the irrational.

You'll no longer want to fix things or wonder what it would be like to get them back and have the relationship that you wanted.

The blame shrinks or completely disappears. You won't blame them for everything because you'll be accountable for your own contribution and focusing on your own efforts to create better relationships.

You'll realise that despite your worries your worst fears haven't been realised, you're OK.

You'll accept the way that it ended and not worry about what coulda, woulda, shoulda happened.

You'll accept the relationship and realise it's OK. You're here, you have a different path in front of you, and because you've accepted, you have the power to adapt your love habits, create boundaries, love yourself, and create a better experience.

During NC when you're very aware of the end of your relationship and a lot of your efforts are focused around making sure you don't get in touch with, or accept contact from, the source of your pain, you will find yourself moving back and forth between the various stages of grief but you will, if you remain committed to yourself and moving on with your life, get to and stay at acceptance. It's not necessarily going to hit you like a sledgehammer and instead it tends to creep up on you and you'll find that you stop resisting moving away from this relationship.

This stage shall set you free. Accept that you will experience the other stages first. Remember that moving back and forth amongst the stages is natural – it is your way of processing what has happened and digesting the reality.

GETTING THROUGH GRIEF

Denial

❖ **Keep it real about the events and the people because you can be objective and move through any anger that results.** It will also stop you from persecuting yourself with blame and shame.

❖ **Deal with your fears.** Whatever you're afraid of, what you do already know is that doing the same things will continue to make you realise your fears. Get them in proportion; don't let them rule you and drive your relationships because it's a big wrecking ball.

Anger

❖ **I cannot recommend Unsent Letters highly enough.** These are an opportunity to write out your feelings and process your thoughts so that you can cleanse yourself of the anger and gain perspective. There's a free and very detailed guide and worksheet available from my site. The chief objection to Unsent Letters is always about it not being 'as good' as telling the person all about themselves but beside the fact that very few people are going to accommodate your desire to pour out your anger on them, you're doing this to help yourself and move on.

❖ **If you don't want to spend a lot of time feeling angry, indignant and screwed over, don't screw yourself over by having little or**

no boundaries. It doesn't work. You already know this.

❖ **Learn to say no and you'll discover the sky won't fall down.** No is not a dirty word. You will simmer with burning resentment if you say yes to everything with the expectation that people will treat you better. Write down what you need to learn to say NO to – these are examples of boundaries.

❖ **Ask yourself what you would do if you were to continue to stay angry?** When I was NC and asked myself this, I couldn't think of an answer. It occurred to me I'd probably think about being angry and wonder if the other person would see the light and yada, yada, yada, and I realised that I wouldn't be doing anything other than stewing in my own anger. That is only going to affect me.

Ask yourself: 'If I'm going to stay angry, what am I going to do?'

❖ **Accept what has happened so that you can accept your anger and come out of the other side of it.** You could fritter away the rest of your days being annoyed and wanting the person you're doing NC on to change but you're trying to control the uncontrollable. Remember – they have their own comfort zone and what you'd like them to be would take them out of that, and clearly they've resisted.

❖ **You will continue to feel angry with this person who has disappointed you if you keep expecting them to do differently to what they have consistently done.** I wouldn't bank on NC making them see the light.

❖ **Forgive yourself.** That means letting go instead of obsessing and getting stuck. If you start being a doer – the whole point of NC –

you'll start to see that you're doing good by yourself, which makes it a hell of a lot easier to let go of whatever has happened and forgive yourself.

❖ **Break the cycle of your anger – deal with your fears, learn to confront situations that make you angry so that you don't feel powerless and berate yourself and lower your self-esteem.** Holding on to and getting stuck in anger is stopping you from embracing your more positive self and we all have one in there that we need to nurture so we can welcome the good in our life.

❖ The key to working through anger is to gain perspective and perspective doesn't come from blaming yourself – it's about owning your own stuff, letting them own theirs, and not doing the whole 'one false move' thing where you think if you hadn't done that one thing, nothing else would have happened. It wasn't all them, it wasn't all you, and the net result is that your relationship couldn't continue.

Bargaining

❖ Don't negotiate with your dignity and don't make bargains based on bullshit. Don't bargain with assumptions that have no basis other than a wing and a prayer!

❖ Some bargaining can allow you to see your way to a constructive solution but make sure it's a constructive solution that has a healthy, uncompromised you in it.

❖ If you have to continue to have your boundaries busted and basically make a radical departure from who you are, you're bargaining yourself into pain.

❖ The best type of bargain you can make with yourself, is something along the lines of:

You know what? I'm going to give myself 3 months where I'm totally focused on me and getting on with my own life and if I still feel a burning desire to be with them after that (you won't), I'll revisit the situation then.

Depression

❖ **What you must remember is that you're human, you love, and you want to be loved. And like everyone on the planet, you don't always do things that are in your best interests and you sometimes do things that you term 'mistakes'.** That doesn't make you a failure as a person and part of the issue of why people get stuck in the anger stage is because they punish themselves by reliving what they think are their 'failures' and wallowing in a pit of blame.

❖ **Support yourself.** Knowing that you're going to feel down for a time is also a heads up to support yourself. Be compassionate and empathetic. Listen to yourself and work your way through the feelings. Allow yourself to feel this.

❖ **You don't have to snap out of it but at the same time as supporting yourself, you have to be willing to recognise where you might be being pulled into something deeper.** This means you may have to keep plugging away at doing normal stuff and resisting the urge to cut off entirely.

❖ **This is a good time to write Unsent Letters.**

❖ **It's also a good time to rely on your support network or reach out**

to find new ones.

❖ **Recognise the blessing in disguise.** Loss is hard but you might be only focusing on one facet of this and not recognising how much you've *gained*. If you only focus on the loss, then you're going to feel depressed but if you look in the other direction, you'll actually see that you have so much to be thankful for and this in itself can represent a turning point.

❖ But most of all, accept that like all of the other stages this stage too shall pass. Keep working your way through accepting the loss of the relationship and you won't act on any bad bargaining ideas.

Acceptance

Even when you reach this stage, you may find that you get caught off guard by feelings or memories. Don't freak out, you're just clearing out.

DON'T SCRATCH THAT ITCH!

UNDERSTANDING YOUR
COMPULSION TO MAKE CONTACT

When I correspond with people who feel a near compulsion to make contact with their exes, they conjure up excuses to send a text, agonise over whether to send a birthday card, worry about what their ex might think about the fact that they are not supposed to be thinking about him/her, and they will have gone through regular periods of cutting contact, albeit maybe more fleetingly. Many people who embark on NC cut contact physically, as in they don't see or speak with their ex, but they remain *mentally* connected by moving into obsessing. This is effectively like conducting your relationship in spirit on an alternative planet.

Obsessing about your ex and analysing the coulda, woulda, shouldas of the relationship is about looking for reasons to blame yourself, which also become reasons to find a way to try to 'fix' things, which in turn also keeps you emotionally invested in the person and the relationship.

Of course, if you are literally consumed by your thoughts and feelings for this person, you'll not only fail to move on, but you'll end up being **trapped/hijacked by your own feelings** and overbusy mind, which pretty much means that your ego is running the show. This situation arises due to chasing unhealthy thoughts (I had a thought so I must feed it with negativity/fantasy) and due to finding it difficult to come to terms with difficult emotions, especially any that open up old wounds. You keep doing things to stem the feelings and thoughts, which keeps you locked in pain.

It's very difficult to gain objectivity, perspective and a sense of reality if you're submerged in an underworld of illusions. You'll feel intrinsically tied to him/her irrespective of whatever pain you've been through and then you'll become convinced that having them in any way, shape or form is better than not having them at all in your life. It's the some crumbs is better than no crumbs philosophy.

And so you will opt back in to the cycle and likely make contact and lather, rinse, repeat until something else happens to cause you to feel like you have to find a way out of the relationship. After opting out, these feelings and thoughts will pop up again and if you keep responding in the same way then you're going to wind up in the same problems despite the fact that you know how this story goes. And lather, rinse, repeat.

Not only will you be trapped by your feelings, often feeling paralysed, unable to do anything or to resist the compulsion, but you may feel *isolated*.

When you're really consumed and preoccupied by a person, very little around you makes sense and it can feel like *this* person has to be reached out to because they're the source of your pain but also appear to be the source of your happiness, plus it seems like they're the only ones who can truly 'understand' what you're feeling. You might reason that reaching out *is* making sense of these feelings (even though it's not) so it's this idea that each time you reach out that you're going to get better and 'strong enough', when actually, it's going to get worse. There might also be this underlying logic that the feelings and thoughts are *about* them hence they're the only ones who can resolve them. This is an avoidance of your responsibility to make sense of your own feelings and thoughts and to also manage them.

You want to *place* your feelings somewhere. You want them to have a *purpose*, an *outlet*, some *meaning* and when something feels so incredibly consuming to you, you can become fixated on doing things that you think will get them to give you what you want or will at least prevent some sort of unfavourable outcome (like being 'forgotten') and then you'll do things off the back of this that you are likely to regret further down the line.

No Contact is difficult. The reward doesn't seem immediately obvious because it feels like you've made a difficult decision and been 'rewarded' with pain. Particularly if you're constantly fighting yourself, you'll struggle to recognise *what* the reward is because you'll perceive the 'absence' of him/her from your life as 'punishment'. You'll associate the feelings of loss and grief with being penalised and particularly if you already have very negative associations with disappointment from childhood or previous experiences, you will struggle with this concept of having to say NO to you. You may feel very tormented by your emotions and thoughts.

Unfortunately by isolating yourself in your feelings, you're putting yourself into emotional purgatory.

When this happens, the likelihood is that you have a habit of validating yourself based on your success or lack of it with your relationships, so when your relationships end, it feels like *you're* broken. You're heavily reliant on external validation so your identity is very vulnerable and you're likely to feel *invalid* when you stop trying to pursue a relationship with this person and will internalise the reasons as to why the relationship 'failed' or the person didn't act as you wanted, turning these into *you* being a failure. You may not even know why you want what you want, you just know that you feel like you want it because of the fact that things haven't worked out in the way that you expected.

217

Being trapped by your feelings and thoughts means that you struggle with rejection and disappointment and in fact may see them as one and the same.

We choose partners that reflect the things that we believe about ourselves, love and relationships, and if we're carrying a lot of negativity, we'll find ourselves with people who exacerbate our worst fears and beliefs. The classic example of this is being afraid of abandonment and then finding yourself with partners who disappear on you or who keep abandoning the relationship and are completely disloyal or who you feel totally insecure around so are constantly afraid of 'screwing up', which leads to people pleasing. The danger in having a lack of self-love is that if we seek validation in others, when we are alone, we'll panic, and quickly try to go back to the original source for some familiarity because we lack personal security and don't have the means to meet our own needs, expectations and wishes.

If you've kept going back to a relationship, you don't know how to, are afraid of, and are unprepared to deal with *loss*. In fact, you may be hypersensitive to loss, and rather than actually work your way through it, you just avoid going the whole hog of feeling the loss. This means that you may have a lot of loss piling up, so each time you experience hurt and loss, it reopens an old wound. This is why it hurts so much and you quickly try to shut down or avoid the feelings.

Avoidance of feeling the pain and professing fear of it, is about dodging the full extent of your feelings and thoughts about the loss, abandonment and any perceived rejection.

Hard as it may be for you to hear, the fact that you avoid feeling something to the fullest extent, doesn't change the reality. The relationship is still over, you still need to grieve it, and you'll still feel rejected, even if it's not actually a rejection of you. However, the difference is that you're prolonging your own agony and suspending yourself in limbo and this is why you'll end up being stuck in an illusion being completely distanced from the reality. You won't see the reality of your ex and they'll recognise this because you need to live a lie so that the reality doesn't pierce it. If you have expectations of them and no doubt communicated this through actions and words, they *know* that you're not being realistic about who they are because if what you expected matched who they *are* not who you would like them to be, you wouldn't be around them anymore.

Burying your feelings as a coping mechanism is shutting down and will affect your emotional, mental and physical health, which has a knock-on effect in terms of how you cope with stress, general life and even boredom.

At times it might feel as if you're trying to swim through quicksand. Plus, while you're 'stuck', they're getting on with their own life or have even moved on with someone else. The more you attempt to avoid dealing with your own thoughts and feelings and the more you keep trying to control the uncontrollable and 'prevent' whatever it is that you think that your feelings and thoughts are telling you, the more pain you end up in. The more exposed you are to being and doing things that you will later come to regard as embarrassing, the more you get sucked down the obsessing rabbit hole because you have an increasing number of things to feel blame, shame and regret about and if you don't force yourself to step back, impose some boundaries, help yourself and even get additional support, this can spiral unnecessarily.

This experience is bringing up something for you that needs to be *faced* and *resolved* in your mind. The thinking attached to whatever it is that this situation is bringing up is contributing to your current position. The way that you see a previous problem is the problem. It's not your worth, it's not that this situation is confirmation that you're an unlovable person or that you 'deserved' previous abuse or that when people and situations don't meet your expectations, it's 'because' of you. The longer that you place other people's behaviour and the outcome of this relationship and even previous situations on you is the longer that you will remain trapped in your feelings and thoughts.

RESISTING IS PERSISTING
UNHEALTHILY

There's a lot of resistance going on. You'll resist letting go, you'll resist getting real, you'll resist accepting the reality of the person and the relationship, you'll resist making decisions, and you'll resist change. Resisting, resisting, resisting, resisting all the way. Resistance is driven by fear and this permeates every single area of your life but it can have particularly disastrous consequences for your self-esteem and your relationships. When you're in a cycle of unhealthy relationships and feeling bad about yourself, the 'familiar uncomfortable' seems more comfortable than the prospect of the 'uncomfortable unknown'.

Unevaluated fears will lure you back into the cycle even though the fear is not actually real whereas the *consequences* of what you've been currently and previously doing *are*.

Being involved with somebody and a situation that runs counter to what you're saying that you want means that you're committed to playing out your beliefs about relationships, love and yourself, which of course results in a self-fulfilling prophecy. Resisting is sabotaging your own chances at happiness because rather than engage with someone when there's a genuine possibility of a relationship and mutual interest while taking responsibility for your own happiness and life, you'd rather keep flogging a dead horse trying to force someone to 'see' you. This is where some of you may become confused because:

1. You believe that you love him/her,
2. You believe that they love you but they just don't know it, or they love you but they're too afraid to show it, or they love you because they tell you that they do even though their actions say otherwise, or,
3. You believe that you have an amazing connection and this is your destiny because the sex is great/they're funny with a great sense of humour/no one's ever made you feel like this before and blah, blah, blah... or,
4. You feel that you love them and if you feel this way then surely they should appreciate how much you feel for them and love you back because you have projected how you think and feel onto them and you believe that you are the best they've ever had, or
5. You believe you can do enough loving for the both of you and that in time, they will realise it and you'll live happily ever after.

Pain is not love, it's pain.

If you've found yourself in the position of having to go NC and have experience of emotionally unhealthy relationships, you have learned the wrong associations about relationships. You think that the feelings created by fear are 'love' and that the excitement and desire you feel is 'love' when it's actually fear. Much of the pain stems from fear and drama and you mistake your feelings of fear and penchant for drama as love, because you have poor relationship habits that have been learned over an extended period of time, often from childhood. This means that your behaviour and desires may seem completely normal and even familiar as you can be playing out subconscious patterns, likely in an attempt to try to right the wrongs of the past and gain validation. What you learn though, as you become aware of your relationship habits and harness your pattern, is that if you don't address how you feel about love, relationships and yourself, your perception of love becomes very skewed.

You learn to accept crumbs, feeling grateful for slivers of attention from people who really don't deserve any more of your time and energy.

You convince yourself that what you're getting is what you deserve or it must be what you want, because surely if you didn't want this person and this relationship then you could walk away?

You believe that the magnitude of pain that you experience is in direct correlation to the amount of love you have, hence the more pain you feel, the more in love you believe yourself to be.

You convince yourself that you're not good enough to expect or get more and that a better relationship will elude you.

You believe that because you have such poor experiences and that time is passing that you must 'settle'.

You become obsessed with getting attention from these people and aren't concerned with the quality of attention so you end up with drama, either sought out or thrown in your direction. Not all attention is created equal!

You become codependent. The very person who is on one hand the very source of your pain, also appears to be the sole source of your happiness. You can't seem to function without them and you believe it's because of your love when in actual fact it's because of fear.

You think that the familiar 'butterfly' feeling that you get around these people is excitement and passion when in actual fact, when you have a habit of being with the same poor partners, it's familiar fear.

You expend so much mental energy thinking about them, what you think they feel and do, what you think you do and feel, the coulda, woulda, shouldas and betting on potential that you lose sight of the reality of them and become obsessed and infatuated with an illusion.

You end up being convinced that obsession and desire to be in control of this person and the situation is love.

Many of the dysfunctional things that happen in poor relationships are easy to bag and tag as 'love' and 'passion' but it's important to remember that reality becomes distorted in poor relationships because it's far harder to stick around when your feet are in reality – you can end up on an entirely different planet!

Fear means that whatever you're currently afraid of isn't happening because if it were, that would be *knowledge* not fear and you'd be responding to that instead.

You may be 'loving' this person because the recognition that certain things aren't happening activates your attachment to this person based on the desire to gain validation. Or you are treating fear as knowledge and not responding appropriately in spite of the fact that what you fear is now happening and needs a healthy response. This is caused by denial, that refusal to accept an uncomfortable truth as fact even though it is.

If you don't reconcile who you think you love with the reality of who they are and the relationship you have, you will fail to process those feelings of drama and fear for what they are – fear and drama – and as long as you're doing this, you'll continue to fall into a cycle of poor relationships that result in similar experiences. Fear and drama make you dependent on surrounding yourself with experiences and factors that make it more comfortable for you to believe that this is how things are. It also causes inaction and you can end up being comfortable with the pattern of the very uncomfortable, because it seems far more uncomfortable to make positive changes that will make you accountable for your own happiness (or misery) and throw the spotlight on where you're expending your emotional energy which may reveal some uncomfortable truths. However uncomfortable these truths may be, the truth will actually set you free if you're willing to face it and deal with it instead of avoiding it.

KEY FEARS THAT TRIGGER THE DESIRE TO RETURN TO THE RELATIONSHIP

Having an awareness of your vulnerabilities as you're embarking on NC means that you can consider an *alternative* and more *appropriate* response to breaking NC, as it would be more beneficial to find healthier ways of responding to these situations than doing what at times can essentially amount to using a hammer when you need a drill.

Identifying the underlying fear behind your actions and thinking is critical because it's a primary driver of your trigger(s). Where you can't identify a clear fear, you can be sure that you are mislabelling, and so treating one trigger like it's another or just using the same default response for anything and everything that you find difficult to handle.

For instance, you might struggle with feeling bored, lonely, afraid and rejected and rather than differentiate between these, you might lump them all together and not really understand your feelings or needs in these situations and then think, "Hmmm, I'll remedy it with some attention" which may be in the form of reaching out or even sleeping with them.

It's a good idea to try to identify where your habit of drama seeking or 'soothing' yourself on unhealthy comforters stems from because repeating this unhealthy pattern of thinking and behaviour can have you repeatedly trying to return to the person or the relationship, even though only hours or days before, you were fully aware of how toxic this involvement was. Suddenly, because you experience the trigger, you're ready to override real concerns and are eager to paper over the cracks or to even attempt to negotiate your way back into the relationship because you don't want to deal with these feelings, thoughts, or even your reality. You basically end up having a relationship with your fear and impulses.

How you respond to these triggers may be rooted in childhood due to experiences such as experiencing abandonment by a parent, and when you get into that zone of being afraid that you are going to be abandoned, or already feel that you have been, it's because something about the situation is familiar, or your overriding fear plays out and you act on it due to not being able to differentiate between now and then, or your feelings versus reality. You end up reliving your fears and experiences while trying to shoot for an alternative ending where you get to right the wrongs from the past. By trying to go back, you're effectively opting back into your unhealthy cycle and you attempt to stem the pain of the breakup by minimising what you feel is the pain of the perceived abandonment. Of course the tricky thing is, is that the abandonment you're trying to stem the pain of cannot be soothed by a painful relationship, especially when you're abandoning yourself in the process.

Abandonment - Fear of being deserted and having to 'fend' for yourself, scared that you're losing them. You're wondering what you did to chase him/her away or scared that you're currently 'scaring' them off. Unfortunately you're highly likely to choose people that exacerbate that feeling of abandonment and everything you are doing is unfortunately just pushing someone who is already flaky even further away.

Boredom - Fear of being unoccupied or 'excited'. When you're in a relationship, this will be fear that everything is going stale and that you need to inject some excitement or else the relationship is doomed. You get nervous when there's no drama, so you may create it, for instance, by ending it to put things back into the uncomfortably familiar. When you're *out* of the relationship, you become afraid of having to be responsible for consuming your own time. Everything has been so tied up in who you are or were when trying to be with this person, that you feel at a loose end and not like an individual entity if you're not with this person or attempting to be. You'll also 'miss' the drama and it may make you feel nervous, agitated and 'bored'.

Feeling neglected - Fear of being unheard, unloved, not cared for, and not needed. Fear that your efforts don't count. Unfortunately even though you feel neglected within the relationship, when you're out of the relationship, you'll seek them out and try to be heard, loved, cared for and needed so that you can feel validated. What's failed to be understood is that NC is symptomatic of the fact that your needs weren't being met when you were *in* the relationship and that you will feel *less* neglected when you step up and discover and learn how to meet your own needs.

Loneliness - Fear of being alone. You're so scared of being alone that you seek solace in people who still make you feel alone when they're in the room with you. You'd rather be lonely in your illusions than trying to

228

rebuild your life with real connections. You'll also find that by being so trapped in your feelings, you'll inadvertently end up isolating yourself. This is why if we make partners our focal point, we end up losing ourselves in them and don't know how to function and be an entity *without* them. We end up codependent and we also make desperate choices in our desperation to avoid the 'loneliness'.

Loss of control - Fear of not being able to control the unfamiliar that comes with stepping out of your [uncomfortable] comfort zone where you know what you're dealing with and by and large know what to expect. Making contact and continuing to try to fit the square peg relationship into a round hole along with managing down your expectations, discussing, trying, analysing, crying, pleading, begging, willing, waiting for him/her and whatever else you can do to hold on because this drama is a 'safe bet'. NC is then associated with the fear of losing control. But you're not in control. If you want to be in control of yourself, your life, and your experiences, you need to opt out of the cycle and cut contact. Until then, you're in *pseudo control*.

Pain - Fear of your tolerance levels, fear that you cannot cope. Even though you spend a lot of time in pain, you're afraid of the pain that you think will be infinitely worse than the current pain you're in. You greatly exaggerate the magnitude of the perceived pain using this as an excuse to avoid change, often confusing the level of pain that you feel with the depth of your feelings, when actually, while part of your pain is grief, part of your pain is also about your self-esteem and how you cope with rejection and disappointment. You also believe that the pain you're in now will be offset by the perceived reward of gaining their love, attention, validation and the relationship you profess to want.

Rejection – Fear of not being accepted, fear that you're not good enough, fear that they hold the key to your worth. You're scared of what you perceive as full-on rejection so you stall the process of grieving and moving on so that you don't end up feeling rejected. This is how you end up returning to the relationship – you're trying to stem the feeling of rejection. If you go back, you think you're not being 'fully rejected', but it doesn't take long until you realise nothing has changed and you're still unhappy.

STOP TRYING TO CONTROL THE UNCONTROLLABLE

You'll send a text, you won't hear back, so you'll send another one. If you get a response, even if it's a short, polite response that conveys no warmth or interest, you'll try to extract further attention and may then try to call or email, or do something to drive your thirst to gain their attention and some level of validation.

Yes you may feel it's better the devil you know, or get a vague comfort from knowing they'll call every seven days, or come back to you when they've been with someone else for 3 months, but the control you think you have is another illusion. *You're afraid of losing control of a relationship and a person that you don't actually have control over.* The moment they go 'off plan', you're going to feel like you're losing your mind... and them.

All of your fears are going to continue feeding into each other and driving you batty until you cut contact and see it through. You're not giving yourself a chance to feel the fear and ride it out. You react to your fear and tell yourself that you're doing it because you're a good woman/man that loves this person unconditionally or that you're fighting for your relationship, or you believe that at least you know what you're dealing with. Unfortunately, no matter what reasons you're under the illusion of, you're engaging in self-depleting behaviour. They're just not *that* special that it's worth going down this road. Find someone who you can keep your dignity with.

When someone wants out of a relationship or doesn't want to get into

231

one, or just is quite simply incompatible with you having your self-esteem in tow, it's a signal that you need to halt.

- If they want to be out of the relationship, why don't you want to be out of the relationship?
- What are they seeing that you're not seeing?
- What are you seeing that they're not seeing?
- If they don't want you, why do you want them?
- If they don't want a relationship with you, why do you want one with them?

You are throwing your love at people that don't want or truly *value* it enough for you to be continuing to give them the time of day. Loving someone doesn't give you an IOU. You're so trapped in your feelings that you've projected those on to this person. You have to realise that what you think, want and need is not the same as what they think, want and need. You can love someone but they don't have to love you back and they don't have to accept your love. If they don't see your love and value it, you're wasting your time.

It doesn't make you invaluable – it makes the situation a no-go.

If you keep throwing your love at people that don't want it and who have the least likely prospects of actually being present and accountable for a relationship, not only are you setting yourself up for rejection, but you're persistently putting yourself in the frontline of rejection and rejecting *yourself*. No Contact will give you back your pride.

Whatever you think is at the end of the yellow brick road of this relationship, i.e., the 'potential' and 'illusions' that you hope to make a reality, it will not wipe out the damage you do to yourself by acting without pride and boundaries.

You've got to feel the pain and grieve the loss of the relationship, the illusions and the person. You'll weep, you'll rage, you'll be inconsolable and maybe you won't eat as much as you should do, or will overeat for a bit, but you need to *feel* the feelings, not shut them down or distract from them with unhealthy behaviour and thinking. Putting off the perceived feeling of rejection, loss and abandonment is prolonging the agony, and numbing you. You have to recognise that yes, you're going to feel some pain in letting go, maybe even a lot of pain, but if you feel it and work your way through it, it's actually only for the short-term.

Your feelings are yours but they shouldn't be running the show.

They're *feelings* not *facts* and while your feelings are yours, they don't come fully analysed and processed so if you don't do the work to understand *where* these feelings are coming from and to also differentiate between how you feel and how things actually are, you won't have enough self-awareness, never mind self-esteem, to support you through even minor difficulties.

Not every thought, assumption or belief is a fact.

The thinking and behaviour that you attach to these feelings needs to be addressed. You will not improve your position and more importantly your sense of self if you don't inject enough self-control to actually think about what you're thinking and differentiate between *ego* and facts. You're preventing yourself from growing. You don't *have* to chase after every thought and you certainly don't have to feed the same repetitive thoughts with the same negativity. You don't *have* to avoid a feeling as soon as it comes up.

The reason you may have struggled to work through the pain before is because you weren't actually working through it. You've been suspended in time and space, wondering if they'll call, when they'll call, what you'll do if they do call, whether you'll be able to resist them, what you'll say, and willing, wishing, waiting and hoping your life away. You've been totally focused on this person, which is really an avoidance of not only feeling the pain, but also working on your own issues so that you don't find yourself in this position again.

BOOBY TRAP - I FEEL SO
REJECTED!

There are two key things that everyone desires and fears in life; acceptance and rejection, and where you don't get one, you get the other. One of the most pervasive feelings you may be left with, either while in the relationship and struggling, or out of it and trying to remain No Contact, is that you may feel the lure of the downward spiral when you believe that you've been rejected.

You will go through a myriad of emotions in the weeks and months ahead, and rejection and anything that stems from it will feel incredibly hard to cope with. When you are feeling like you've been rejected, discarded or turned down by the object of your NC, it may provoke you to:

- Turn the perceived rejection inward and be full of self-hate / dislike and blame.
- Obsess about the finer details of your relationship, analysing it and looking for further reasons as to why you were rejected.
- React to the feeling of rejection by seeking them out to validate you so that you can feel less rejected.

The first thing that I want you to keep in mind, and make part of your focus, is this: **Instead of thinking about what you perceive as rejection, ask yourself what it is that you're rejecting about *this person* or the**

relationship? Your sense of 'rejection' can often be very much tied to the good times and feeling that you must have done something really awful to scare him/her away or that if only you had tried harder, been better, needed less, been accepting, turned a blind eye etc, they wouldn't have 'rejected' you.

The scary thing is that you may already recognise on some level that this isn't somebody that you should remain involved with due to the sheer impact on your self-esteem, but the confusion and rejection kicks in because you can't understand why someone who doesn't deserve your time would reject someone 'like you', because you know you're better than being with someone who would have you in this position in the first place... and yet you're not currently interested in someone who *would* actually treat you better because now the person who you perceive as rejecting you appears to be so much more 'valuable' because they're rejecting you.

There are a number of reasons why you may feel like you're 'unacceptable', 'not good enough', 'worthless' or even 'rejectionable' but here are some of the most common that I've come across:

- Because you felt very deeply for this person and it wasn't reciprocated or appreciated.
- Because you put up with what you would normally regard as unacceptable behaviour and it *still* didn't get you the relationship you wanted.
- Because you feel like you dared to trust this person far more than you have anyone else and you got burned.
- Because you feel that you were very much yourself with this person and that it wasn't 'acceptable'.
- Because you weren't yourself with this person and it *still* wasn't 'good enough'.
- Because you changed to be what you think this

person wanted or needed you to be and *that* still wasn't good enough.

- Because you silenced your needs, expectations and wishes, even when your soul ached and you felt as if you were being suffocated and you *still* didn't get the love and the relationship you wanted.

- Because you knew that this person wasn't a healthy choice in relationship partner and you in fact knew that you were compromising your values and that this person wasn't even worthy of your time and yet... they're treating you like *you're* not worthy of *their* time.

- Because you tried very hard and it feels like nothing was good enough and this may even remind you of when you were a child.

- Because this person said things about or to you that cut right to the heart of your worst fears.

- Because this person said things that you know aren't true and yet you're doubting yourself.

- Because it feels like this person gave a better relationship in the past to someone else or that they're now being the person or giving the relationship that you wanted to someone new.

- Because it reminds you of previous rejections and even though they may not be the same, you treat them all similarly.

- Because they're similar to a parent/caregiver who rejected/abandoned you.

- Because you're convinced that you did something to 'make' them behave a certain way or for the relationship that you thought was on offer to be retracted and that you've not been given enough of a chance to make amends.

- Because your entire life and identity was based around this person or what you hoped that your relationship would be and now it feels like you have nothing.
- Because you sacrificed your family/friends/health/work/aspirations/interests and hobbies.
- Because you were willing to discount your own perception of things and may even have cut off or even attacked anyone who challenged it or your ex and you.
- Because you're hurt and disappointed and you associate and equate these feelings to rejection.
- Because you don't like and love yourself (self-rejection) so if they don't, it's a double-whammy.

No Contact neutralises/minimises the compulsion to react to the perceived rejection because if you don't feel your feelings, process the loss and use the distance and space to gain objectivity and *perspective,* responding to this sense of rejection will open you up to further pain. The horrible thing is that the 'rejection' can always be minimised, but in continuing to engage in the hope they will change, that they will finally recognise your worth, it instead gets *compounded.*

Think about this: If you allow every single interaction with partners and dates to inform your identity, and those people are unhealthy partners who may take advantage of or even abuse you, you'll be left with very little self-esteem. In taking on their baggage along with your own, they end up leaving you with some of theirs when they go. This is why it will feel as if you're losing a piece of you when it's over because they're the source of your value and until you learn to like and love yourself, perspective is missing. It's also critical to recognise that the type of person who tends to require NC isn't rejecting you but they *are* rejecting what they don't want to be or do, including:

Having to love
Having to communicate
Having to be emotionally available
Having to care
Having to empathise
Having to recognise someone's needs other than their own
Having to trust or be trusted
Having to be relied upon
Having to be respectful
Having to recognise and respect your boundaries
Having to be committed
Having to be expected or needed
Having to deliver on the words that come out of their mouths
Having to make an effort
Having to think and be conscientious with integrity.

Can you truly say, hand on heart with no equivocations that this person has rejected *you*? How did they get this power? *Why* do they have this power? Every single one of these reasons I listed earlier for why you feel rejected point to either the other person's behaviour (which isn't about you), or people-pleasing behaviour (which would mean you weren't being you *anyway*), or giving someone power that they *don't* have and aren't entitled to in the *first* place.

If feeling rejected is about the other person's behaviour which *belongs* to them, they're not rejecting you. Their actions are not an indictment of your worth and you're not 'provoking' it. I'm not suggesting that you haven't possibly at times provided a fertile ground for them to overstep the mark, but this isn't *new* behaviour orchestrated *specifically* for you; it's *character* driven and in *existence.*

If feeling rejected is about this person not being or doing what you expected, wanted or needed in spite of you engaging in people-pleasing behaviour, they're *still* not rejecting you because you weren't being you *anyway.* How can somebody reject who you are and were, if you weren't being this anyway and were effectively wearing a mask?

If feeling rejected is about you *deciding* that this person has the power to determine your worth or is about *giving* away power, they're still not rejecting you in the way that you think because the only place they have the power to determine your worth is in your mind where *you* attach meaning about your worth to their actions. Self-worth is *self*-worth.

Now I'm not saying that there isn't an element of feeling rejected when a relationship ends, but for the sake of your own self-esteem and keeping the amount of bullshit in your life to a minimum, don't get things twisted and assign *your* power and perception to another party. *Disappointment,* which is your hopes and expectations not being met hurts, but it's important to realise that disappointment is not the *same* as rejection; they're two entirely different things. Your hopes and expectations are *yours* and ultimately we *all* have these going into and during a relationship, but the fact that reality doesn't live up to them is not about your worth as a person and is very much about whether the relationship had the content and the legs to go the distance.

BOOBY TRAP - SEEKING
VALIDATION & UNDERSTANDING

If you're struggling with rejection, you're also struggling with validation, which is seeking confirmation of something. What you have to be asking yourself though is: Why does this person have all of the power and understanding to prove *your* validity, *your* worth, *your* perception of the relationship and *your* truth?

If you look closely at where you've taken a detour from your identity and personal happiness, you'll see that where there's been struggles, there's also been a consistent thread of trying to be understood and validated via people pleasing and being over-empathetic. The result: you probably feel *mis*understood, *in*validated and are living off crumbs in an atmosphere of never feeling sure of yourself, all while hunting for something that can be found a lot closer to home.

A people pleaser and an unhealthy relationship are a toxic mix that poisons your life especially when post-breakup, you're *still* trying to please this person in some way so that you can feel better, which might give you a short-term 'fix' but leaves a longer term hangover. You are more concerned with a perceived 'reward' than you are with the impact of what pursuing their validation is doing to your sense of self.

Our society has taught us that it means something about us if our relationships *don't* work or that we mean a hell of a lot more if we're in one whether they're working or not. When you're a people pleaser, the suppressing of your needs, wishes, expectations and basically *yourself* means that when your relationships end and you may recognise the sheer

241

necessity of NC, you feel bereft. This is due to not knowing who you are, not knowing how to meet your needs, plus you may still be looking for others to step in for you where you're not stepping up for yourself. Hence you end up contradicting your own desires and wondering if you expected too much or whether you could downsize your expectations to make the relationship work.

NC starts to feel 'wrong' because *you* don't approve of you not people pleasing and it feels as if you're feeling 'bad' all of the time. Er, you didn't feel too hot when you were in the relationship people pleasing *either*.

In your world, because you spend so much of your time suppressing who you are to meet other people's needs, wishes and expectations even if they run counter to yours, you regard opting out as *aggression*; getting your needs, expectations and wishes met by *force*. It's why you may feel as if you're a 'bad person' and may be tormenting yourself with guilt because you feel as if you're doing something 'bad' now that you're not there to participate in Groundhog Day #734. Yes you are asserting yourself by sticking up for your own boundaries and withdrawing from this cycle, but you are *not* trying to *force* them to meet the needs, wishes and expectations that they haven't been meeting *anyway*. All you're doing is following through on the breakup.

Another easy way back into an unhealthy dynamic is to tell yourself that you *need* to continue engaging with this person because you won't be able to move on until they understand your perspective or where they've 'gone wrong', or what they've lost. You don't want your relationship to end and for the person to move on and not show some sense of struggle with their conscience, identity or actions because *you're* not moving on because you're going through these very struggles seems wrong. You determine that you'll feel a whole lot better if this person could *just* see things your way and admit their errors. You fear calling it 'done' in case 'understanding' would have meant a solution to 'making' this person do what we want, need and expect. The outcome of moving on is often attached to achieving *full understanding* of the other party or the relationship, as if less than 100% but more than a code red alert is grounds for reasonable doubt.

"Tell me that I'm not crazy!"

"Tell me that I didn't misunderstand!"

"Tell me the truth because I know you lied but I won't be able to accept that you lied until *you* accept that *you* lied".

"Tell me that it was all your fault."

"Tell me that it was all my fault."

"Tell me that you're sorry."

"Tell me that because you know what you did, that you're suffering and you'll be suitably pained until I feel better about me."

"Tell me that you finally understand all of the things that we've talked about in our hundreds of discussions where you never understood me before."

"Tell me that you're a narcissist or sociopath or that you've got some mental health issues that I've been reading up about on the internet".

"Tell me that you wish you'd been a better man/woman in the right time and place to be with a wonderful person like me".

Sometimes you want to make sense out of nonsense. Often you're pretty much trying to get a Ph.D. in another person's behaviour.

Respectful relationships and breakups rely on *empathy*, which is the ability to put ourselves in another person's shoes and see things from *their* perspective. This is very different to what many people engage in – *over-empathy* – putting ourselves in the other person's shoes and seeing things from *our* perspective, which neglects reality. We think about how *we* see things, how *we* do things, what we would do if they were the other person, or how we imagine we might react if we had someone who was practically throwing their love at us, or even what we think we might need if we had the same problems that they do. This perspective tells you about *you* and maybe what might happen in *your* version of an ideal world, but if this person is not the same as you (they're not), you're missing out on valuable information that's being used as a basis for dodgy decision-making.

When you're giving yourself a hard time about doing NC and not getting the validation and understanding you need, you're actually hating on yourself for the fact that they're *now* not doing something that they weren't *ever* doing anyway or that they only pretended to do for a time.

Some of these people have the compassion of a stone, some live on Me-Me-Me Island, some just can't see past their nose never mind their penises/vaginas, and some will mirror you when trying to get what they want. It's about *their* needs, *their* wants and *their* expectations. In some circumstances, they may be entirely unaware of the true extent of your feelings – for instance in a one-sided crush or relationship – and really, it's nigh on impossible for him/her to truly validate you. It's also safe to say that some circumstances don't really allow for a person to put in as much time and energy as you'd like into investigating 'what happened' and closure because from their point of view, they have plenty going on in their own lives and may have already made the decision to avoid their feelings or even to move on with someone else. In fact, they may already have done their closure. Alone.

You might argue that it would benefit you both because you'd get validation and they'd be a 'better person' due to the insights they gain while providing you with this understanding and validation plus this outcome could be avoided in their future relationships or even with you because maybe you could give things another shot. This is all a rather presumptuous fantasy and this argument and grand masterplan ultimately originates out of you trying to make this person – an external 'solution' – solve *your* internal issues.

Looking for validation and understanding is something that's counterintuitive to doing NC. How are you supposed to cut contact, take care of yourself, grieve your relationship and begin to heal and move on if you're still looking for something from that person and the relationship?

A need to be understood becomes a *reason to make or accept contact*. You want them to 'get it'. You want them to 'see' you, to 'hear' you, to recognise your value. The more validation and understanding that you seek, the less positive validation that you get and the more questions are left unanswered, especially if you're doing things that harm you emotionally. In cutting contact for whatever reason, this means that the relationship in whatever form it took is now over. If you weren't able to get the validation that you think you need from this person *before* you went NC, you are unlikely to get it now. Even if you do get some level of validation, like many before you and many who will come after, you're likely to find that it falls far short of what you expected you'd feel like when you got it. This is because the validation you actually need now that you've gone NC is from *you.*

Get behind your decision to cut contact so that you provide yourself with the validation. A breakup isn't a democratic decision and neither is NC. When you break, you *break*. For the type of validation and understanding that you're looking for to happen, they would have to understand not only what the issues were that led to the failure of the relationship, but they'd also need to have genuine love, care, trust and respect, along with the willingness and supporting actions to change for their *own* benefit, never mind yours. That's just too much stuff that's out of your hands so you have to get back to you.

BOOBY TRAP - LURED BY NOSTALGIA

You can end a relationship with damn good reasons, feel empowered and relieved, and then, the high wears off and BAM!, nostalgia beckons and if it's allowed to overtake reality, you will convince yourself back into the relationship, likely using a fantasy of magical fixes as the basis.

Nostalgia is why people who have experienced severe abuse go back to their dangerous relationships. The very relationship that torments them can suddenly seem like paradise in comparison to having to face their life without this person who may have compromised them so greatly, they have no sense of who they are and their capabilities. Abusive relationships aside, nostalgia is why so many people not only break NC but they stay in relationships that aren't working or go back to them, or even remain in a relationship based on the first days/weeks/months that they knew a person, even if much more time has gone by where they have shown themselves to be very different and they're actually in love with the memory or illusions of that person.

Nostalgia tends to kick in when people are actually making real progress and it's as if they become fearful of moving forward and so they try to turn back. Nostalgia can also be a response to fear, not knowing how to sooth, when for example, one is bored or lonely, or it can be down to another relationship prospect not working out, or just the natural pangs of missing this person. All of this is normal. Distance gives objectivity.

It's understandable to feel a sentimental longing or wistful affection for a past that you have happy associations with but, and it's a big but, by placing too much emphasis on these associations, you may forget about some more compelling *negative* associations that should keep you *away* from the fantasy. Whether you focus on 'good points' or you seem to have selective episodes of Relationship Amnesia, taming or even neutralising your amnesia will protect you from opening yourself up to further pain.

Most relationships have 'good times' and 'good points' although it's not unheard of to remain in a relationship where the 'good moments' only lasted for all of a nanosecond. When you become hung up on these 'parts' of a person (or the times) which are treated as being more valuable than the whole, you end up minimising or even flat-out disregarding everything else because it contaminates your vision and plans.

Focusing on these 'points', you can put aside 80 or 90% of things that render the relationship a no-go because the 10% looks so attractive. It's the false belief that the '10%' indicates what they and the relationship *could* be and that the other 90% can be 'solved'. Unfortunately, if what makes up the remainder is what constitutes NC, it's an unhealthy relationship. There are plenty of people who have been in an abusive relationship where for instance, they don't get beaten every day but they do get beaten from time to time – that's unacceptable. Once out of the relationship, nostalgia's easy because you conveniently forget about the gnawing worry, the watching your p's and q's, the insecurity, the whole people pleasing and sometimes living on a knife's edge not knowing whether to expect a hot or cold phase.

NC can be a struggle because buying into nostalgia helps to avoid the truth.

NC doesn't mean that your ex doesn't have these aspects to them that you value so dearly but the truth is, you *overvalue* those good points and good times *because* you are struggling with less palatable aspects. If you were being more realistic, yeah you might still have your nostalgic moments but you'd moderate them with the truth before you got sucked down the rabbit hole of making contact.

When your ex is able to play the 'nostalgia card', it's because they perceive nostalgia to be your 'hook'. They know that you have the relationship equivalent of anterograde amnesia, *relationship amnesia*, where you seem unable to recall more recent events beyond a particular nostalgic point in time where you're 'stuck'. This enables them to press the *reset button*, which is where they try to pick up from where they conveniently think that they left off. They'll conveniently forget all of the shitty things that have happened during that time and will just think that they can swoop in and say, "I miss you" and shazam, pants down. They know that you would have told them to jog on long ago if you were more realistic.

A nostalgic ex is very reactive and plays to the nostalgia hook when lonely, bored, in need of an ego stroke, they have to fill time in their schedule, or they want to be reminded of that feeling of talking to someone who adored them no matter how much they effed up. When they flick through their mental Rolodex of people who are most likely to respond to their 'efforts' they think of you. At some point, the backtracking begins by which time they may already have called or texted but they won't let you know that the situation has changed. When you respond and they don't meet your expectations, you're left feeling confused, possibly very hurt, possibly feeling as if you've been pranked.

Really what you've experienced is called *Failure To Think Shit Through*. You've got to stop expecting change. *You've* got to be less reactive *also*. You can only fall for the same con more than once if you're being reactive and excessively optimistic based on a fantasy. You need to sort out your relationship amnesia.

Nostalgia causes loss of perspective but is also interpreted as a cue to chase a feeling.

You'll let your mind wander, you'll remember the great sex on that weekend away, or that time when they said that they could see themselves getting married to you or swigging drinks in Shady Pines nursing home together, or when they told you that you're the only person that understands them. The yearning will kick in and you'll want to feel like you did *at that moment*, instantly forgetting the bigger picture and how you felt over the majority of the time.

Relationships aren't about trying to recapture the good times; you're supposed to be treating each other with love, care, trust and respect as well as living and loving together. You don't have to keep trying to put the past on repeat and *living* in the past if you have a relationship in the *present* to work with.

You allow yourself to get caught up in nostalgia and to let them essentially use your own history to disarm you *because* of these positive associations that you have but, you're forgetting that you also have *negative* associations and one costs you more than the other. Nostalgia in itself needs to be your cue that you need to practice being more in the present and to connect with what is happening in your life *now*.

You may feel nostalgic but NC stops you from letting your feelings and imagination run the show, especially as you become increasingly aware that you don't have the *real* relationship to substantiate these feelings and wishes.

NC, in teaching you to be self-aware and to be responsible and accountable, helps you to also become aware of the *negative associations* that this relationship represents. It allows you to see the wood instead of just the trees and it doesn't take away from or even destroy the happy memories you may have of this relationship, but it also helps you to make *sense* of it all. When you break NC to rekindle positive associations, you end up adding to the negative association bucket. Part of the grieving process *is* remembering the good times but also reconciling what you feel with the big picture and letting go.

It's not about censoring yourself from remembering the good but if this is the *only* thing you focus on, it removes perspective, making it easy to falter with NC because you're obviously not thinking about what your motivations were for doing NC in the first place. Each time you allow nostalgia to blind you, you end up engaging in bullshit thinking that may lead to bullshit decisions that then lead to bullshit actions which will open you up to hurt and regret that can be entirely avoided, *especially* if you've fallen into this nostalgia trap before.

Nostalgia also provides a window into understanding yourself better and recognising where you can step up and meet your own needs, expectations and wishes, but also what you may want in a future relationship or even showing you where your blind spots are. I hear from people who feel nostalgic because when they were with this person, they felt so alive and full of plans. They miss what they thought that they were going to do or how they felt at certain times.

You can feel alive, you can have new plans, you can create these experiences in your own life both alone and with someone else, and your ex isn't the *only* person on the entire planet that you can experience this with. They're not.

When you're in the midst of a relationship, it's difficult to see these lessons clearly but when you're *out* of it and NC, when you're doing your best to come back to earth and move forward, you have the space to gain the clarity that you need. NC will neutralise the effect of the nostalgia so that it's in its rightful place, not overtaking your 'controls' and keeping you living in the past or betting on potential in the future. It's understandable to feel sad for what you've lost or even what you *think* you've lost, but all is not lost and actually, these relationships prove to be blessings in disguise that connect you with your authentic self, so don't feel *too* sad as you may miss out on the undoubtedly better opportunities ahead.

BOOBY TRAP - GREAT EXPECTATIONS

In order to come down from the lofty heights of your illusions back to earth, it's important to quell the sense of rejection, the desire for validation and understanding, and the lure of nostalgia with a reassessment of your expectations because it's not adjusting or managing your expectations, whether that's of you or partners, that repeatedly sets you up for disappointment.

Expectations are about having a **strong belief** that something will happen or be the case in the future and as with any belief, you align your thinking and behaviour around this, which may under- or overestimate yours or the capabilities of others. Behind every expectation are *other* beliefs and if they are unhealthy and/or unrealistic, you may be setting yourself up for a fall.

Once you embark on NC, unmanaged expectations can cause you to:

1) Expect things to be easier and less painful than they actually are or to expect things to be much harder and more painful, which basically sets you up to fail.
2) Expect too much or too little of yourself.

3) Expect this person to do things in the way that you've mentally worked out.

Having a level of realism is something that while you can argue that it means that you'll have to accept what may be some uncomfortable truths, it also makes for a far less stressful NC journey overall. Whether you convince yourself that it's going to hurt too much for you to be successful at it, or you embark on NC thinking that what you feel when you're on a high from standing up for yourself is going to last forever more, these expectations mean that you're being unrealistic, which opens you up to thinking and doing things that are likely to come back to bite you later.

It's going to hurt.

I could lie to you and tell you that this is going to be a piece of cake but I would also be lying to you if I said that this is going to be hell on earth although it's possible that you'll have moments where you do think that it is. The reality is somewhere in between the two. Some days will be harder than others but the truth is, if you embark on NC without game playing and by focusing your efforts on taking care of yourself, the net result is you will feel much better than you feel 'bad'.

Yes making the decision to go NC may be a big one for you and very painful *but* that doesn't mean that because you've made this decision that it's job done and should be happy days from here on in. You didn't get into this relationship in a hot minute and it's totally understandable that if you've emotionally invested *and* had some difficult experiences *and* you're feeling bruised in some way then yes, it's going to hurt. It's not going to hurt forever or even for a very long time but it is going to hurt.

Optimism is good but be careful of being so optimistic that you're not being at least a little realistic about the road ahead. It's not about forecasting doom (which is pessimism) but you can be optimistic and at the same time be aware of your vulnerabilities so that you can consider your plan A and plan B should these situations arise. On the flipside, planning for failure isn't going to help you either because if you don't believe that you can do NC, you won't. If you believe that you're going to give it everything you've got and that if you get knocked down, you'll get up and live to see another day and try again, you're in a better mindset. Expecting this all to fuck up is saying, "I don't believe that this can end because I don't believe in myself." It doesn't matter if you've struggled before – you can learn from these experiences and the 'mistakes' and bumps along the way are part of the learning curve to eventually making a success out of it.

You also have to recognise where you open yourself up to pain by expecting people to be or do certain things that are not in their character or their values. By evaluating your expectations, it helps to manage disappointment or to even avoid it, but you can also end up planning for success instead of quietly or even openly expecting this not to work out.

The trouble is that not all expectations are realistic.

It *is* realistic to expect to be treated with love, care, trust and respect within a relationship but it's *unrealistic* to expect that someone who isn't actually consistently behaving this way 'should' behave this way or that they will and 'should' give you the relationship that you expect because of *your* feelings and *your* hopes and *your* expectations. It's not unrealistic to hope that somebody will be interested or that if they reciprocate your interest that it *might* turn into a relationship, but it *is* unrealistic to expect that because you have feelings that it most definitely *will* turn into a relationship where this and that will happen and you'll both ride off into the sunset. I think it's realistic to hope that you will see somebody again after sleeping with them but it's unrealistic to think that it's going to become a relationship or that they're The One because you had a great date followed by even better sex on the first night. It *is* realistic to expect that a relationship that you're putting your effort, emotion and time into should go somewhere but it's unrealistic to expect that relationship to go somewhere if when you remove what you're doing, there isn't much left, or you're engaging in unhealthy behaviour within an unhealthy relationship.

Bearing in mind that expectations are based on beliefs, it's not uncommon for people to find themselves in relationships where they expect to get screwed over, often because they recognise on some level that they're with the type of person who is likely to screw them over based on some of their predictive behaviour *or* because based on their own self-worth and attendant beliefs, they just don't believe that a relationship with them in it is going to go somewhere.

Be careful of using unhealthy and unrealistic expectations to set yourself up for a fall.

Whether you expect too much or you expect to fail, you're going to be hurt and disappointed. If you expect too much, not because your expectations are 'wrong' but because it's too soon or because these expectations don't make sense with that person's behaviour or even your own, that's a recipe for pain. If you expect to fail, if you expect for it all to go to tits up, that's *still* going to hurt because it will feel like confirmation of your worst beliefs and because you will have pursued a fantasy of *not* failing at the same time without truly supporting it with the healthy beliefs, actions and relationship.

You wanted this relationship to go somewhere. You *expected* this relationship to go somewhere... even if you had *other* concerns that meant that deep down, you didn't really *believe* that this could go where you expected because you were aware of the issues that no doubt contributed to you having to do NC. You might have wanted to be wrong about them. You might have hoped that what you perceive as a 'mistake' would come good.

It's entirely understandable to be hurt during NC because breakups hurt anyway and then when you have go an extra step with NC, it can feel as if the process contradicts every thought, feeling, hope and expectation you ever had for this relationship and it can accentuate this sense of rejection.

How can I be going NC when I thought that we were going to be together forever?
How can I be going NC when I truly believed that he/she meant every word they said?
What if by not going NC I have the chance to not be disappointed?
What did I do to deserve this disappointment?

Many people confuse disappointment with *rejection*. In fact many equate one with the other, but the fact that you've experienced disappointment doesn't mean that you've been rejected or that your expectations are or were 'wrong'. This disappointment didn't happen because you're not 'good enough'; it happened because there were a number of contributing factors very much separate to your 'quality' as an individual that together meant that your expectations couldn't be met.

It's the end of your relationship, which is the emotional, physical, sexual, spiritual and mental connection between you both. The relationship while it had these two physical beings in it that were interacting with one another, this *connection* between you both that makes the relationship is in itself intangible and can be ended by words alone even if physical, emotional etc, evidence remains. It's confusing and painful because so many feelings remain along with hope, expectations and plans and then, it's over and there's white space to fill and that space hurts and that hurt may feel like rejection but it's not; it's disappointment.

Whether they said or did things to create those expectations or you arrived with them anyway irrespective of who they were or the quality of your relationship, or you got carried away with assumptions and fantasy, you had expectations and NC is partly about reconciling those with reality, grieving the loss and learning positively from this experience.

THE NATURAL CONSEQUENCE OF AN UNHEALTHY DYNAMIC OR WAY OF BEING *IS* NC

The reason why NC is so effective at communicating your boundaries and your newfound or *re-found* self-respect, self-love, self-trust and self-care is that until you cut contact, you're so 'there' they assume you're there for them to do what the hell they please with. You're so *there* in mind, body and spirit, they don't get to 'miss' you but more importantly, they experience little or no consequences. The first time they may truly *value* you and recognise the consequences of their actions is likely to be when you value you too much to want to go back there.

Life involves making choices and accepting and rejecting behaviour. It's important for us to feel perceived and genuine differences in behaviour and circumstance for us to truly feel the impact of consequences.

If someone learns that no matter what they do, you'll be there, they learn that there are no consequences to be felt and in essence, what they're doing becomes acceptable. It also means that they don't fear losing you because they don't think that they're *in* a position to lose you. It's only by consistently demonstrating that you're no longer 'there', that you can effectively convey a different message to someone who has learned over time that you're 'reliable', albeit for the wrong reasons. This isn't about getting this person to 'miss' you so that you can get back together; NC communicates that it may have been a long time coming, but you *do* have boundaries, there *are* negative consequences to what has happened between you both, and that the access or the privileges that they've previously enjoyed have been revoked.

Each time you stand firm in your NC position while also treating yourself with love, care, trust and respect, you learn *healthier* responses to what have previously been tricky situations for you. Being able to sit through your feelings, to talk yourself out of breaking NC, to remind yourself of the reality as opposed to the illusions and essentially not falling for the same con numerous times keeps you in the present instead of living in the past or betting on a potential that's already let you down. If they want someone to get an ego stroke, shag, a shoulder to lean on, or whatever it is they need, you're *not* that person so they need to jog along to someone else.

The litmus test of all this is, if you develop a healthier relationship with yourself, which will result in healthier beliefs about love and relationships, will you still want this person? Will you still love him/her? Will you still be breaking your neck to see when you can next make contact with them? Unlikely. If you have a pattern with this person or a general pattern of unhealthy behaviour and thinking in your relationships, it's time to make the choice that if loving someone means that you can't love, care, trust and respect yourself, *always* and with no equivocations, choose you.

MOVING FORWARD

STAYING FOCUSED

No Contact means that you have to go cold turkey but at the same time you're also putting yourself in the driving seat of your life, creating your own closure, and are starting to gain self-control in a dynamic where at one time you probably thought it was impossible. Maintaining NC can be hard but it's nowhere near as hard as the alternative – selling yourself short and being unavailable for an available, healthy relationship. You're only going to do NC and move on *happily* if you nurture yourself through this time. This is not a time when you need flog yourself with judgement, blame and shame – you need to have your own back and *love* yourself through NC and if you don't love yourself that much right now then you need to learn to *like* you during NC.

Several months into being NC from my ex, I discovered for the first time that I genuinely liked and loved myself. This was incredible progress considering that NC had felt like torture and I hadn't believed that I'd make it through it. I'd lost my self-respect over the years (I'm not entirely sure I even had it in the first place) and when I finally started sticking up for myself in a positive way (not sticking up for myself by demanding that this clown leave his girlfriend and shack up with me), I became comfortable in my own skin and far more compassionate for this person I'd been who massacred herself in her involvements.

Nurture yourself. This is about putting yourself first and you need to do it because you've allowed their needs and inability to give you what you need and want to be placed at the centre of your universe. Be the centre of your own life.

❖ **Don't overwhelm yourself by thinking about getting through months.** Take it a day at a time, then a week at a time.

❖ **Mentally pull over and come back to earth.** When you feel compelled to break NC, it's important to do the mental equivalent of pulling over on the roadside and refocusing your thoughts. Where are you? What is the reasoning behind your desire to break NC? Based on previous experiences and what you know of this person, what do you know is likely to happen? When you get hurt, can you deal with the medium-term repercussions? How will you feel after you have reacted? Think about it. What's the choice here? You don't have to choose the path of least resistance. You are in control of yourself, not your ex or your urge to break NC. You are behind the wheel of your choices so make sure that you choose the right path for you.

❖ **Be powerful in your own mind.** They are not better than you and they do not have the power over you that you think they do. You are powerful, you can do this; believe it. Willing NC to work is not enough – you have to do the actions to support the process and also support those actions with the thoughts to back them up. Don't hope you'll be able to do NC, plan to be able to do NC and do the work to make it happen.

❖ **Challenge yourself not to think about this person.** Day one, each time you think of him/her, mark it down on a sheet of paper in your diary or something. Total it up and the next day, aim to do less by getting into the habit of directing your thoughts elsewhere and being more focused on your present. Or if you're really hung up it might be better to do it by week. Target yourself to reduce it down each day/week. The trick is that if you are focusing on yourself and feeling in a better place emotionally, your thoughts will be directed away from this person. Set yourself a challenge. I've practically had to sit on my hands in the past to get to the end of first week, but once I did it, it became a challenge to get to the end of week two and so forth. I rewarded myself along the way and when I got to three months, my shoe cupboard had a new arrival…

❖ **Plan your weeks, especially in the early months.** Keeping really busy is a great way to learn how to deal with boredom and stress as well as an opportunity to do things that you're interested in or to reconnect with friends and family.

❖ **Work out your short (under six months), medium (6–18 months) and long-term (18 months+) goals.** This exercise is invaluable because it makes you identify and acknowledge your needs, wants and expectations. What you do from now on has to genuinely align with these goals if you want to be authentic and happy. If what you're engaging in takes you in a different direction, you're short-changing yourself. These goals give you a focus and a purpose because much as the process of NC is important, you also have to get on with having a life at the same time.

❖ **Keep a journal.** You're going to learn a hell of a lot about yourself during this process and a journal is a record of what happens during the process as well as a resource when you're having an off day or week and need a reminder of how far you've come. Many readers incorporate goal setting but they also use the journal as a means of keeping themselves accountable and learning to write out their feelings.

❖ **Keep a Feelings Diary.** You can incorporate this into your journal or do this separately or alone. Identify what it is that you're trying to avoid, whether it's uncomfortable feelings, or having to deal with a particular situation, such as moving your life forward after a breakup. Keep a record of what has happened on days where your feelings for your ex intensify and keep a note of when and why you hit despair – here amongst the feelings by which you're being hijacked, lies the truth. Find it. Also learn to recognise the cues and triggers that are most likely to affect you including recognising when you're in the zone of feeling vulnerable to breaking NC. This gives you an opportunity to reground yourself and invest your energy into more productive uses. Grab the worksheet from http://bit.ly/ncfdbkk.

❖ **Put on your favourite feel good/empowering song, turn the music up loud, and verbally vent out your frustration.** Sounds crazy but it's great for releasing pent up emotions and you start to get a sense of humour about the whole thing. Oh and your neighbours can't hear you talking to yourself. If you're crazy like me, you'll do a little dance too. When I was NC, "I Used To Love Him" and "Forgive Them Father" from The Miseducation of Lauryn Hill, along with "Since You've Been Gone", Kelly Clarkson, "In The Morning", Mary Mary and pretty much anything by Beyoncé got me going. Alanis Morrisette's "You Oughta Know" is genius.

❖ **Write 'Don't call {insert name}' on a Post-It and stick it to your phone, mirror and anywhere else that helps you visualise.** Or write it in lipstick/wipeable pen on your mirror. I know of people who literally littered their homes with messages and it works.

❖ **Some people need reminders of the 'Big Whoppers' – the horrible things that they did.** Type up the short form of each offence and print it out in a decent sized font. For example, 'Stood me up six times'; 'Never delivered on any of his/her promises'; 'Broke up with me when I was sick in hospital/my parent died', then stick it up somewhere that you can see them. Or create a screen saver…

❖ **Note the memory triggers.** I only had to think of 'The time with the panic attack' or the name of a place or the phrase, 'You know my situation' to remember how poorly I'd been treated. Keeping a note of these are reminders of why you won't be going back.

❖ **Take a break from dating.** Dating Hiatuses enable you to reconnect with yourself and heal but they also prevent you from knee-jerking into another dubious relationship due to trying to avoid your feelings. Most importantly, if you're not dating, you won't end up in a situation where you're comparing a new partner or getting a knock back which then triggers nostalgia for your ex, which in turn you may respond to.

❖ **Be careful with alcohol.** If you're the type that calls/texts your exes when you've had a few vinos, it's probably best to cut back until you've gotten over the urge.

❖ **Use the time to reconnect with other aspects of your life.** Friends, family, hobbies, work. When we're messed about, something always gets sidelined so use the opportunity to get things back on track. Apologise to those that you need to, although you'd be surprised how pleased people will be to have you back. You're not the first and you won't be the last to get lost in a relationship but use this time to remind yourself of the things that matter because if you base everything around one person, when they're no longer in your life, you'll feel bereft and lost, which adds to the sense of dependency. If your friendships and family relationships are under strain, you may find that this is a time where you not only reinforce your boundaries, but you focus your energies on building your life and making new connections.

❖ **Ask yourself, 'What am I not prepared to accept in a relationship?' so that you can define your boundaries.** If you can't think of something, you know something's really, really wrong, because we can all find at least ten things that are a serious no go for a relationship! Just look at the chapter *40 Signs That NC Is A Necessity – that's* boundary inspiration. If you accept everything that comes your way, how would you make the decision to opt out?

- *What should you be saying no to?*
- *What do you want to say no to right now but can't get the words out?*
- *What makes you feel miserable and taken advantage of?*
- *What are your consistent negative threads (your patterns) in your relationships and what has it taught you about what is and isn't acceptable?*

❖ **Ask yourself if you're a 'yes' person** and what you could cut back on to begin reducing your Nos. Start small and build up. Assertiveness is like a muscle. The more you use it, the stronger you get at assertiveness tasks. Start with one a day and then increase every few days to a week. It can feel painful initially but that passes when you realise how good *you* feel.

❖ **NO isn't a dirty word!** Life is not about being a yes person and rolling over so you can be walked all over and kicked while you're down. Being in a relationship is not about being a martyr! The word 'NO' allows you to respect yourself... and for others to respect you. Nobody can say yes all the time and regardless of whatever warped messaging is telling us the contrary, nobody expects you to say yes all the time... unless they're an assclown.

❖ **Don't make exceptions to your boundaries.** Decide what they are and don't deviate. You don't need to decide to bust your boundaries because someone says the right thing. Keep your boundaries *and* let them say the right thing and let it proceed from there. At least you know that you're continuing authentically.

❖ **Don't do things for approval.** If you wouldn't do it if you didn't think that they would reward you with something that they may not even be aware of, don't do it. If you wouldn't give something if you didn't think that you would get something back, don't do it.

❖ **Are you pretending to be happy and grimacing your way through life?** You know when you smile but it's a tight one, or the smile doesn't reach your eyes because you're in turmoil within? What is bugging you? Be honest and then think about how you can best reduce the impact of these stresses even though it will take you out of your comfort zone. Do what makes you happy and start by saying and showing *no*.

❖ **Do you have boundaries in other areas of your life such as with family and friends?** If so, what can you apply to your romantic relationships?

❖ **List your potential boundaries that have arisen through your introspection** – you'll find that a number cross into each other and can be summarised into one boundary. The likelihood is that you should be able to find at least ten things that are major Nos for you.

REBUILD A LIFE WITH MEANING

How much of your life have you spent waiting for their call?
Can they call you up and you agree to plans at the drop of a hat?
Do you have a limited social life but are saying that you don't meet people?
Do you spend a lot of time on dating sites but not actually out there in the real world?
Are you not deviating from a routine that you've had for a long time?
Do you think every romantic prospect you meet might be the one?
Have you isolated yourself from family and friends?
On the occasions when you're out, do you worry about getting home for their call?
Are you staying home at the weekends feeling sorry for yourself because you feel you have nothing to do because you're not with someone or they're not around?
Do you assume that everyone else is in relationships so you can't hang with them?

You have a life. Right now it's a life that's based on a romantic partner whether you have one or not. When you're with someone, they're the focal point of your life. When you're not with someone, the fact that you're not becomes the focal point of your life. NC is an opportunity to build your life in the way that you would prefer it all while being your authentic self. I'm not saying that you need to be roaming the streets looking for a partner or that there's anything wrong with wanting a relationship but make sure you know the difference between wanting and *needing* due to a relationship being critical to your identity.

If the routine you've had for five years, the places you go etc means that you've met a handful of people in that time, it means you need to change your routine and add flavour and variance, and even a bit of spontaneity. You've got to be in it to win it. You're not going to meet somebody if you never leave your house. If you have a pretty rigid routine with very little deviations in your social life, you're less likely to meet somebody and are pretty much relying on someone to land in your supermarket basket or on your desk or on the treadmill. Yes you can try to meet people online but you need to be personally secure to do so and be prepared to do due diligence because you have to wade through a lot of people that talk out of their bottom to get to the genuine folk and you also need to be less swayed by words and illusions in order to recognise a decent relationship prospect.

If you want to like and love yourself, start doing things that add to your life and make you feel good. Sex and romantic partners, or the possibility of these two things are not the only things that can make you feel good. If you fill up your life with meaning and plans, this will bolster your confidence and sense of self which makes you happier, which also gives off positive vibes, and will find you in situations where you're more likely to meet someone who vibrates with a more positive you.

Irrespective of what sex you are, as human beings, we feel more confident about having a relationship with someone who believes they're an entity who has cultivated a life of their own.

It is daunting to be around someone whose only life is you. It screams codependency and this is not attractive and will have you taken advantage of by the wrong types of people. This is another reason why NC is so effective. It says 'Actually, I do have a life beyond you!'

❖ **Do the things you want to do now.** Do not put off enjoying your life until some far off date in La La Land when you hope to have a man. Don't let men eat up your good years! You don't get back this time and I know that the day I made my life about me, my health, self-esteem, confidence and life immediately changed for the better.

267

❖ **Get out there and grab life.** Take up hobbies, try them out, discard them, join clubs, take a class, eat where you want, do a marathon, whatever. Grab life!

❖ **Make plans for your week instead of hoping someone will come along and make them for you at the last moment.**

❖ **You *have* to create a social life otherwise... you'll do nothing or half-heartedly accept invites.** Put a calendar on the wall or in your phone so that you can see what you're doing and fill it up.

❖ **Read your local paper or check out local sites.** My favourite resource to recommend is Meetup.com. It's transformed the lives of so many readers. Search for meetups in your area by interest or just sign up for something. The great thing is that you get to practise hanging out in groups and getting to know people without an agenda. Also check out eventbrite.com, Time Out (also the mag), and a hell of a lot more. There's also a plethora of interest-based sites so get on them and out there. Whilst it's not for everyone, if you like eating out, try one of those dinner dating sites, or look at dating events based around interests. I know that you can go on mystery walks and do outdoor stuff with singles. Yes there may be a few cringey moments, but you'll be getting out there.

❖ **Try stuff and go along for the hell of it.** You never know, you might like it. If not, leave and try something else next time. The more things you try, the more likely you are to find regular things you like.

❖ **Keep your head up and be open.** Don't go to the effort of going out and then hide your head or be standoffish. I know it's harder, particularly for shy people, but challenge yourself to have small conversations starting out. They don't have to lead to anything; just chat for the hell of it.

* **Accept invitations that you wouldn't normally accept.** I nearly turned down going to a charity event on a Saturday night with my friend and then changed my mind. I figured that I needed to seize the day and have a laugh. That night I spotted someone buying drinks at the bar and playing backgammon at one of the games tables. We're still going strong and married with two lovely daughters! He hadn't planned to go either but thought he should just go for a laugh! We actually don't know if we'll enjoy something and can often be cautious due to confidence or being close-minded. I've had a lot of great nights out, but I've also had some dodgy ones, but at least I was out living life!

* **Organise things with your friends.** Married, attached or single, have fun with your mates. Dinner parties, hanging in the park, going to the movies, will give you a sense of feeling nurtured plus they're likely to invite you places too because they'll realise that you want to be social. Don't judge your friends on their relationship status – my closest friends are single so it's not the case that attached people don't want to hang out.

* **Volunteer, start going back to church, do a course, do a taster course, go to wine tasting, go along to company events, go along to client events, travel, go to the next town up or into the city.**

I get it. You want to love and be loved, wake up to someone, have someone to share your life with and basically do what couples do. But if you continue to look for someone to complete you, you'll put yourself in the position of automatically feeling incomplete. You'll look at what you

269

don't have while forgetting what you do have or could have if you valued what you did have. People who don't value themselves, their own time and their own lives are not happy because they rely on other people to create that value. They decide that until they have someone, they're not valid, that being single is that annoying time to pass between partners, and don't realise that life is passing them by while they're focusing on the wrong things.

I'm glad that I learned to like and love myself before I met my now husband. I love my life with him and our children but I still have my own life and there are things that I do for myself to make myself happy, as opposed to relying solely on him or things that we do together to make me feel happy.

When you do meet someone, you need to be a fairly secure individual so that while you're obviously going to find your lives blending, you still have your own interests to draw on and have the ability to make yourself happy. This *can* be you and when it is, you won't sideline yourself, your own interests and the things that mean something to you to be with somebody, because you'll be able to have these *and* the relationship.

YOU MAY FALL OFF THE WAGON
BUT JUMP BACK ON IT

It's possible that you may fall off the wagon. It's possible that you already have. You won't be the first and you definitely won't be the last. Don't beat yourself up over it but get back on the No Contact saddle. Sometimes we need to fall off the wagon to learn more about our ex and ourselves and cement the decision to cut contact. It's obviously not ideal but I wouldn't go losing your mind over it or give up on NC – when somebody knows which buttons to press, they'll press them. Familiarise yourself with what those buttons are so that they are no longer your Achilles heel and you can recognise when your ex is playing to these supposed 'weaknesses'. Use the memory of feeling horrible to empower you to ensure you don't fall in his trap again, but don't beat yourself up over it – you are human and part of that is sometimes making errors in judgement.

It doesn't matter what it is that breaks NC, just as long as you get back on the wagon and *keep going*. It may set you back a little but it is likely to strengthen your resolve. The fact that you've broken NC doesn't mean all of your previous efforts are a waste. They will play their own part in cumulatively contributing to your future success. Believe.

You are human. You love and you want to love, and sometimes, you will seek it out from the wrong people and situations.

All you can do is learn from your experience so if you do fall off the wagon, no matter how big or small the fall is, use what has happened to cement your knowledge and understand what you're doing. Learn from your efforts so far and recognise where you faltered, listen and support yourself.

- ❖ **Don't turn a temporary setback or even a moment in time into a permanent judgment and way of being.** That's catastrophic thinking.

- ❖ **Don't turn it into an episode of mass proportions.** You can make this as big or as small as you want this to be and I suggest you opt for the latter.

- ❖ **Do make sure you assess what it was that triggered the 'fall'.** Were you bored? Were you being nostalgic? Had you had a confrontation with someone else that left you vulnerable? Had you slid back into denial temporarily and got really hopeful about them? Whatever it was, identify it and have a plan of action for how to deal with next time round.

- ❖ **Remember that you now know that the fire still burns.** Note what happened, how you feel, what you hope for, the reality of who they are and remind yourself of why things haven't changed and that it cannot be the relationship you want. Remember this feeling. Write it down and do not forget what you have felt in the aftermath of the fall.

- ❖ **Strengthen the barriers to communication.** Block their number, filter their emails, cross the other side of the road, return their stuff and basically do whatever you need to do to shut them out.

- ❖ **Don't feel like they got one over you and have had the last word.** The last word is action because the next time they come slinking around expecting you to be there, you won't be.

❖ **Use this time to remind yourself of exactly why you're NC and renew your commitment to yourself.** Refer back to the chapter, *40 Signs That NC Is A Necessity*.

❖ **Focus on your own life.** Make sure that you're filling it with things to do, places to be, friends, family, work and other things that you can draw pleasure from. Probably best not to let yourself get too bored at the moment as you're likely to let your mind wander and give yourself a hard time.

❖ **Don't be too hard on yourself.** Learn the lesson while loving yourself at the same time and *move on*. What can I do next time? How can I learn from this? Find the positive lessons, find the growth. The lesson is not that you're weak or a bad person. Keep thinking that and you'll be falling off the wagon again, not because you are weak or bad, but because who the hell has the strength to do very much when they're mentally running themselves down?

❖ **Accept that it is normal to have urges to be back in the relationship that's not working for you or to crave the person.** It's not abnormal; it's a natural part of the process. Acknowledge them but don't chase them and if anything take a few moments and do an awareness check. What else is happening in my life that is causing me to react in this way? What am I avoiding? What is reminding me of this person or triggering the urge? Then find ways to manage these triggers. It may be stress, it may be seeing the same coloured car. When you realise what is triggering the urge, it loses its power because you see that it's not some divine intervention telling you to go back to the relationship. Remember that the urge passes – you won't get to discover this if you knee-jerk into making contact. Ride it out and each time you do, the urge will last for shorter and shorter periods.

****

Remember that you're not striving for 'perfect NC'. Anything that goes well or doesn't is feedback that will help you to move through this process and make decisions that treat you with love, care, trust, and respect. Trust yourself and trust the process. Don't trust the insecurity.

But most importantly no matter how much they beg, no matter how much they plead, never feed your ex after midnight. Just joking! But no matter what, cut the contact. No Contact isn't about finding out what they will do when they lose your supply of attention and adoration and then panic; it shouldn't matter what they say or do because you want this person out of your life, regardless. You have so much more to offer to yourself. One day it will dawn on you that you're no longer NC and that you're just living your life. Until then, *trust* the process and you'll gradually learn to trust yourself. You can do this! You've got this! *Believe.*

You can grab resources like *The Unsent Letter Guide* from my site www.baggagereclaim.com.

4106549R00158

Printed in Great Britain
by Amazon.co.uk, Ltd.,
Marston Gate.